THE AGE OF
SHAKESPEARE

THE AGE OF SHAKESPEARE

Frank Kermode

Weidenfeld & Nicolson

LONDON

First published in Great Britain in 2004
by Weidenfeld & Nicolson

Originally published in the USA by Modern Library
a division of Random House, Inc

A CIP catalogue record for this book
is available from the British Library.

ISBN 0 297 84881 X

Typeset by Selwood Systems,
Midsomer Norton

Printed in Great Britain by Butler & Tanner Ltd,
Frome & London

Weidenfeld & Nicolson
The Orion Publishing Group Ltd
Orion House
5 Upper Saint Martin's Lane
London, WC2H 9EA

Frontispiece: William Shakespeare; the Chandos Portrait
(Courtesy Mary Evans Picture Library)

Contents

Prologue: The Age of Shakespeare

One remarkable aspect of the period we know as Elizabethan (sometimes, for convenience, the term may be extended to cover the earlier part of the Jacobean period) was the development of a professional drama.

The venues of earlier popular drama had been makeshift, as when inn-yards were adapted for use as theatres, but in the later years of the sixteenth century London acquired purpose-built theatres that could accommodate audiences of up to three thousand. These theatres were owned mostly by men who formed companies with structures not wholly unlike those of the old craft guilds, though Shakespeare's company was somewhat apart from the others, since in time the members of the company came to own the theatres as well as the plays. The 'sharers' commissioned the plays, owned them, acted in them, and, in the case of Shakespeare, wrote them. Some of the partners, including Shakespeare, became men of substance, property owners with handsome incomes, but that was a later development; in the early part of Elizabeth's reign, theatrical performers were still thought of as tumblers, strolling players, vagabonds.

At a time when most poets had to depend for their living on aristocratic patronage, often grudgingly provided, the theatres of London, with their huge appetite for plays, gave many of them employment as dramatists. They often worked in haste, and with collaborators – occasionally a different writer for each of the five acts of a play. How many plays were written in the relevant period cannot be exactly known; G. K. Hunter, the best authority, says that between 1558 and 1642 there were about three thousand, of which six hundred and fifty have survived. It is an old story that many were destroyed in the eighteenth century by a cook in the employ of the scholar Bishop William Warburton, who used them to make pies. It is the figure of three thousand that is important, and if it is roughly correct we can say that plays were written at the rate of about thirty-six a year – or more, if one allows for the fact that the theatres were closed for quite long periods.

It seems clear that in a time when new styles of commerce were being developed in the burgeoning London finance and commodity markets, this was another new kind of business. The pay was quite good, and more certain than the vagaries of patrons. The companies were not entirely self-regulating; indeed, it was possible to carry on this business only under the protection of a nobleman, a court official. The need of protection was real, if only because the City of London was an inveterate enemy of the players. Consequently, the theatres had a unique social situation. They had to please the multitude yet avoid upsetting potentates at court who scrutinized their texts. With the hostile City they had to deal cautiously, for the City authorities disliked them, not only out of a puritanical mistrust of plays but also because these authorities had to deal with occasionally troublesome audiences and with traffic congestion outside the theatres.

There was a convenient pretence that the job of the licensed companies was to perform on command at court; their activities outside that preserve were officially counted as rehearsals. But public performance was essential to profit, and they operated in some of the roughest parts of London, notably among the watering holes and brothels of the South Bank. As time went by, different social types came to prefer different kinds of entertainment, and that demand was met at one end of the scale in the big down-market public theatres, and at the other in private indoor theatres, where, until about 1609, the actors were boys. Out of such diverse enterprises a fair number of men made a good living and kept in easy touch with the whole society of the time, high and low.

I shall try in what follows to keep in mind that just as his was only the grandest of the companies, Shakespeare was only the grandest of the poets writing for the many and various audiences who were in effect his patrons. He was, under one aspect, a very successful businessman, a type that was common at the time in other professions; but he was also a poet who had certain aristocratic contacts and, as a liveried servant of the Crown, a minor courtier, one who eventually had his own coat of arms – a man acquainted with much that went on in social ranks both above and below him. During the twenty-odd years of his career, the status of actors was greatly enhanced; he was not the only theatrical man to receive a grant of arms, nor was he alone in making a good deal of money.

It was now for the first time possible for an actor-playwright to do so. In 1572, when Shakespeare was an eight-year-old in Stratford, a statute was enacted concerning the proper punishment of 'rogues, vagabonds, and sturdy beggars', a class held to include 'all fencers, bearwards, common players in interludes...not belonging to any baron of this realm'. The next few years saw many tracts – mostly, though not all, Puritan in inspiration – against the theatres. Opposition continued throughout Shakespeare's career and beyond; but since he and his colleagues enjoyed official protection, popular success, and the possession of considerable property, charges of vagabondage were never likely to disturb him. His company occasionally got into a little trouble with the Privy Council, but even then Shakespeare's name does not appear among those who underwent examination.

1. A panorama of London, by Claes Jansz Visscher, circa 1600. *(Courtesy Bridgeman Art Library)*

2. Sketch of the Swan Theatre, by Johannes de Witt, circa 1596; the only surviving drawing of the Elizabethan period showing a stage and actors. *(Courtesy Mary Evans Picture Library)*

3. Portrait of Queen Elizabeth I (1533–1603), by Marcus Gheeraerts, circa 1600, painted during the queen's visit to Blackfriars. *(Courtesy Bridgeman Art Library)*

4. Portrait of King James I (1566–1625), by Daniel Mytens, circa 1616.
(Courtesy Mary Evans Picture Library)

The first task of one who sets out to write briefly on Shakespeare and his age must be to move the focus back from the life of the playhouse and say something about the greater world of national politics. One dominant concern in that world throughout the Tudor period was the precariousness of the royal succession. If this now seems a relatively remote and unimportant matter, it is worth recalling that Shakespeare's history plays, a good quarter of his entire output, dealt with anxieties, indeed with civil wars, about succession, and even portrayed the events leading up to the dubiously valid accession of Henry VII, Queen Elizabeth's grandfather. The succession was a matter of concern to everybody, not only because the monarchy then had more personal power than it has been able to keep, but because in Tudor times the whole issue was bound up inseparably with religious differences, and religion could mean war. The expansion of the empire under the Protestant Elizabeth inevitably caused conflict with Catholic Spain and allowed her the triumph over the Spanish Armada; but there were still English Catholics who had been instructed by the Pope that Elizabeth was an illegitimate usurper and that one could be forgiven for eliminating her. The plots against Elizabeth of her cousin Mary, Queen of Scots, and Mary's Catholic followers were a serious recurrent anxiety.

By the date of Shakespeare's birth (1564) Elizabeth had been on the throne for almost six years, and the 'Elizabethan Settlement' had established the Church of England as Protestant. Though 'Anglo-Catholic' (to apply a later description), the English church was now entirely severed from Rome. The events that brought about great changes in English social and economic life had occurred in the reigns of Elizabeth's father, Henry VIII, and of his son Edward VI. It is traditional to say that the 'English Reformation' took place from 1529 to 1559 – the latter is the date of the Elizabethan Acts of Uniformity and Supremacy, and the former the date when Henry, failing to obtain the Pope's consent to his divorce from his first wife, Catherine of Aragon, made himself supreme head of the Church in the Pope's place. This neat formulation overlooks the history of dissent from Wyclif and the Lollards in the late fourteenth century, a reform movement not forgotten in the years before Henry's catastrophic break with Rome. But that break, and the proclamation of the English as the true Catholic yet vernacular church, was, despite opposition, decisive in the long run.

Henry very much wanted a male heir, but the surviving child of his first, supposedly invalid, marriage was a daughter, Mary. His second wife, Anne Boleyn, produced another daughter, Elizabeth, and it was Jane Seymour, the third of his wives, who gave birth to a son, Edward. He succeeded his father in 1547, and his brief rule was dominated by a harsh Protestant regency. His successor, his elder half-sister Mary, was, like her mother, a devout Catholic and did all she could to restore relations with the papacy. Her too-late marriage to Philip of Spain was barren. At the end of her short reign she was succeeded by Elizabeth, who resumed her father's title as supreme head of the church, and was able to withstand both the Catholic and the growing Puritan oppositions.

The Reformation affected not only theology and liturgy; the distribution of national wealth and political power was greatly altered by the dissolution of monasteries and other rich ecclesiastical establishments. The upheaval affected not only the clergy; ordinary people had to accommodate themselves to radical change. Historians argue about the exact nature of that change. We used to be taught about the 'waning' or the 'autumn' of the Middle Ages – a story of loss, or at least of a late flowering that preceded loss. An age had ended when most people derived their religious knowledge not from printed books but from the imagery and symbolism of the wall paintings and stained glass of the churches, a huge non-literary context for the Catholic sacraments (immemorially seven, but now reduced by the theologians of Reformation to two). It used to be taken for granted that those old-fashioned ways of worship and instruction had become self-evidently obsolescent. The Roman church had permitted all manner of abuses as well as forbidding translation of the Bible, the Word of God, so that by the time Reformation arrived it was badly needed. Now there are historians who dispute this account of the matter, and lament the rapid extinction of the old faith and its attributes – its arts and rituals, its control over the pattern of life over so many generations.

This is in part the thesis of Eamon Duffy's remarkable book *The Stripping of the Altars: Traditional Religion in England c. 1400–1580* (1992). Duffy emphasizes the degree to which almost every aspect of daily life had been consonant with the liturgy, and the ways in which religious doctrine was taught – not only by pictures but by many liturgical acts not properly part of the Mass – instances of traditional piety, as when the episodes of the Passion were annually re-enacted by the clergy but also, in dramas of their own devising, by the laity. For example, since St John spoke of the parting of Christ's garments, two linen cloths were removed from the altar at the appropriate moment. A sepulchre was prepared in which the Host was reverently laid – for of course the Host was literally *corpus Christi*, the body of Christ. And such enactments should be borne in mind when one reflects on the extraordinary persistence of quasi-dramatic traditions throughout the entire period before the professionals began, in the new world of the later sixteenth century, to absorb and secularize play-acting and translate it from these quiet devotional origins to the inns and theatres of London.

The commercial development of drama was one more sign that the world as regulated by liturgy was being supplanted by a world more concerned with capital and labour – a world in which time itself had a different quality. 'The rhythms of the liturgy,' writes Duffy, 'were the rhythms of life itself.' The rhythms of work and of pleasure reflected the routines of liturgy and prayer. The doctrine of Purgatory, which the Reformers especially detested, had for centuries exerted a powerful influence on conduct, whether in the ordinary course of life or on the deathbed, and its hold over people's minds remained strong long after it was condemned, in ways well illustrated by Stephen Greenblatt in his *Hamlet in Purgatory* (2001).

Duffy's account of the stripping of the churches – the altars were now considered idolatrous and were replaced by 'communion tables' – emphasizes the tragic aspect of these losses. Dissident commentators dispute his contention that in the period just before the Reformation the Catholic religion, far from being in decay, was indeed in a perfectly healthy state. Of course a case can also be made for the beneficial effects of the new Protestantism, and indeed some say that the notion of undisturbed Catholic contentment suddenly and barbarously interrupted by Reform is mere propaganda. The intellectual and educational achievements of Protestantism, it is argued, are in the Catholic version of events much undervalued. So is the fact that throughout Elizabeth's reign Cranmer's *Book of Common Prayer*, containing not only his celebrated prose but also the Articles of the reformed Church of England – various in number but eventually settled as thirty-nine – defined the differences between Roman and English doctrine and could be consulted in every parish church. Also to be found in the churches were the Great Bible and Foxe's *Acts and Monuments* (1563), better known as Foxe's *Book of Martyrs*, powerful propaganda for the true (English) Protestant-Catholic faith, and for the royal and imperial claims of Elizabeth. The book remains notorious for its polemic against Rome and the Marian persecutions.

These books in part replaced the old images – wall paintings, stained glass, rood screens, decorated altars – of the old regime, and, to judge from the growing strength of Protestant feeling, their effect was, in its different way, as powerful. One estimate holds that in 1585 the population of England was five per cent Catholic and fifteen per cent Puritan, the rest accepting the middle way prescribed by Elizabeth. Such estimates are of course just more or less well-informed guesses. There was certainly a rump of faithful Catholics, but England in the time of Elizabeth should probably be thought of as primarily a Protestant nation, at war ideologically as well as militarily with Rome.

Both sides were equipped for international conflict, not least as to the war of ideas. England had theologians like Cranmer and

Jewel (defender of the antiquity of the English Church), while Rome used such propagandists as Cardinal Borromeo, whose apologetics became well known in England when distributed by Jesuit missionaries. Shakespeare's father seems to have owned a copy of Borromeo's *Spiritual Testament*, a guide for perplexed and oppressed Catholics. In the active as opposed to the contemplative life, the age is famous for its seamen pirates and for the secret services that employed such gifted spies as Christopher Marlowe. There were some, among them the poet John Donne, who hoped for a theological compromise, believing some move towards reunification might be possible, but the differences, for instance those concerning the doctrine of the Real Presence and the celibacy of the clergy, were too stubborn to be reasoned away.

Orders relating to the nature of divine service and attendance at church were now issued by the state, replacing the older priestly sanctions that were backed by the authority of Rome. Above all, the vernacular Bible, long denied to the Catholic laity, was now made the foundation of faith. The reformed church believed it had gone back beyond a millennium of papistical distortions and rediscovered the true Christian message of the New Testament. It is not surprising that some lay people, especially those born under the old regime, might cling almost unconsciously to the religious practices of their youth. Moreover, there were bitter factions within the Reform movement, and the extremists tended to gain ground, zealous in the detection and destruction of anything that could be labelled idolatrous.

They had no time for such festivals as Corpus Christi, instituted in 1264 – a feast of central theological importance as a celebration of the Real Presence in the sacrament, but also the occasion of great civic festivities, including the cycles of plays organized and financed by the craftsmen's guilds of the towns. Of these remarkable works the 'mystery plays' of Coventry, York and Wakefield are the most famous ('mystery' was a word for 'trade' or 'craft') and they continued into Elizabeth's reign. Shakespeare as a child could well have seen them at Coventry; but by his time they were frowned upon. The feast itself was no longer legal, and the expense of these elaborate displays had probably grown too great, and so they expired.

These productions had a didactic purpose, offering in the vernacular a long series of plays about sacred history. Events in the Old Testament were presented as prefiguring the truths of the New (much as church glass and paintings did, or had done), together with scenes from the lives of the Virgin and Christ. Performances were on 'pageants' or carts, stages that could be moved from one site to the next. As far as possible, each guild chose a subject appropriate to its particular mystery. Costumes were elaborate, and there was some use of stage machinery. Solemnity was mixed with broad humour, and some stock characters became famous – when Hamlet tells the travelling actors not to out-Herod Herod, he is alluding to the traditional rant of that character in the Corpus Christi plays. Spectacle was provided; hell yawned and devils vomited smoke. Some of the plays are more subtle than this account suggests – the Wakefield (or Towneley) *Second Shepherds' Play* is renowned for the daring of its double-plotting, mixing the serious theme of the Nativity with farce – indeed, the kind of mixture to be found later in some of the plays of Shakespeare's contemporaries; for a celebrated example, see Middleton's tragedy *The Changeling*.

The mystery plays testify to the ingenuity of their authors

and actors, and also to the strong desire of late-medieval Englishmen to *perform* their beliefs, to act out in their own persons the sacred truths as they had been taught them in sermons and paintings. These plays translate into their own popular style the patterns and narratives of medieval piety; and they were fun, occasions for holidays. They prove that the English had long been well attuned to dramatic display, whether as actors or audience. These tastes were inherited, in very different circumstances, by their descendants. A common purpose had brought together the variously gifted craftsmen of the town, and they made a solemn feast into a universal holiday. But they could not survive the threat of Reform forever. That they lasted so long is a tribute to the staying power of the old style of popular religion even when powerful forces were at work to destroy it.

For a time it had seemed possible to retain much of the old way of life while acquiescing in the new. Henry VIII himself remained attached to much that was traditionally Catholic, and up to the date of his death in 1547, people could keep to their old ways. Mass was celebrated with impunity. Elizabeth, when her time came, had a fondness for some old habits and customs, and favoured compromise and moderation. When she was excommunicated, threatened with assassination, and opposed by the great Catholic powers, she adopted a more severe, more warlike attitude. Nevertheless she wanted the English church to be a *via media* between Rome and Calvinist Geneva. The difficulties of the situation – between hostile Rome and burgeoning Calvinism – are well illustrated by John Donne's 'Satire 3', an excited, disturbed reflection on his own need to choose (he was brought up a Catholic) that must have been echoed by many intellectuals of the time.

Between the reign of Henry and that of his younger daughter came those of Edward and Mary. Edward's counsellors were hardline opponents of Rome, and through them he condemned all 'papistical superstitions' such as rosaries, holy water, prayers to the saints, ceremonial candles, fasting, indulgences, relics, and the existence of Purgatory. Edward was probably predisposed to the Protestant cause by the influence of his father's sixth and last wife, Catherine Parr, a devout adherent of Reform, and as he grew towards maturity he became as fiercely Protestant as his advisers. So the confiscation of the treasures and the estates of religious foundations was continued so energetically that it is described by the historian John Guy as 'the largest confiscation and redistribution of wealth since the Norman Conquest'.

The transfer of ecclesiastical wealth into secular hands brought great changes in everybody's way of living. Not surprisingly, it was sometimes called plunder. An early protest was the 1536 rebellion called the Pilgrimage of Grace, a serious but rather innocent affair that Henry easily suppressed. In 1549 there were widespread riots, often motivated by need, for despite its access to new riches, the Crown overspent on defence, and the poor were growing poorer. Such protest movements tended to originate in the north of England, where Catholic nobility, gentry, and commons, still bound together in the old faith, wanted to halt the defacement of their churches and to contest the heresies of those in London who were responsible for such practices.

According to Eamon Duffy, the Catholic religion still flourished with all its old vigour into the 1540s. But the depredations continued, the wall paintings covered in whitewash and roods and altars smashed with axes. The new Prayer Book

(1549 and 1552) mentioned above is now valued as beautifully written and inseparable from the central Anglican tradition, but at first it was much resented, partly because it abolished many traditional feast and fast days, and there must have been many older people who longed to go to Mass. It is noteworthy that the great musicians of the Elizabethan church, William Byrd, Thomas Tallis and John Bull, all remained Catholic, having perhaps a special dispensation to do so. Byrd even wrote music for secret and illicit celebrations of the Mass.

Protestantism, at any rate in most of its manifestations, was a religion of the word, and it was an old complaint that the gorgeous polyphony of much Catholic music obscured that word; these aural delights were now as suspect as the colour and ceremony of the old liturgy. After many vicissitudes they would be partially restored in an Anglican version, but were again opposed and eliminated in the revolution that ended the life and reign of Charles I, and the life also of his 'High Church' archbishop, Laud. The Puritan forces that ended absolutism in 1649 were gathering force at least a century earlier.

Edward died at sixteen in 1553 and was succeeded, against Protestant opposition, by his Catholic sister Mary, whom he had tried but failed to convert. Her determination to restore England to the Catholic faith is usually regarded as the cause of a reign of religious terror, though Duffy claims that 'men breathed easier for the accession of a Catholic queen' (503). Mary imposed a somewhat modernized version of the old faith, for example exploiting the power of the printing press, as Protestants had done, and making available printed Catholic prayer books. But she is remembered for the persecution of her opponents rather than for her attempts at 'creative reconstruction'.

Given the religious upheavals produced by Edward and Mary, it would be strange if people were not still somewhat muddled in 1558, when Elizabeth succeeded to the throne. There were strong inducements to accept the rules of religious observance as promulgated from London. To opt for recusancy was to take a possibly dangerous and sometimes costly stand, at a time when one risked a fine even for failure to go to church. Some kept the faith despite the penalties; some presumably did so without advertising the fact; and others, perhaps the majority, lived more or less contentedly, betwixt and between.

There was an obvious connection between the religious and ecclesiastical events sketched above and the matter of the Tudor succession, with its grave bearing on foreign relations and on public order. Henry VIII's need of a male heir was partly responsible for his divorcing his first wife, officially on the ground that she had previously been married to his brother. Consequently Mary, the child of this technically incestuous and illicit marriage, was a bastard in the eyes of Reformers. Elizabeth, the product of what they regarded as the king's illicit union with Anne Boleyn, was in Catholic eyes both a bastard and a usurper. Scholars laboured to demonstrate that she was nothing of the sort, and that the church of which she was now the head was the true, primitive Catholic church. Her European enemies could not be expected to agree, and it may be that there were others, to borrow a phrase from Evelyn Waugh's biography of Edmund Campion, who did not 'find it probable that the truth, hidden from the world for fifteen centuries, had suddenly been revealed to a group of important Englishmen'.

The political and religious difficulties arising from uncertainties of succession would not go away. Mary married Philip

II of Spain, son of the Emperor Charles V, to whom she had earlier been betrothed, but achieved only a phantom pregnancy. Her right to the throne was at the outset disputed by Protestant supporters of the unfortunate Lady Jane Grey, a grand-niece of Henry VII, who was proclaimed queen but lasted only nine days, to be ousted by Mary. She met the usual fate of losers in this game. However, Elizabeth's accession passed without immediate disturbance – there was at the time no other plausible candidate. She was expected to do better than her sister, and so was given a warm welcome in London. Protestants hailed her as the English Deborah, after the prophetess who for forty years assured good government in Israel.

Elizabeth was twenty-five, a learned young woman, with some tenderness towards old religious practices. She had a fondness for ritual, used candles (deplored by Edward) in her chapel, and kept up the custom of washing the feet of the poor on Maundy Thursday (the day before Good Friday). As a girl she had had the benefit of instruction by great humanist teachers such as John Cheke and Roger Ascham. She wrote and spoke French, Italian, and Latin with fluent ease. Late in her reign she surprised some Cambridge professors who insisted that on their territory it was not permitted to speak English by making a powerful impromptu speech in Latin, and in the same language delivered a formidable reproof to an impudent Polish ambassador. Her addresses to her parliaments are impressively intelligent, dignified and authoritative. In early life she had lived quietly in seclusion, though not without danger and sometimes under house arrest; she was also imprisoned in the Tower of London on suspicion of her having had a part in a plot against Mary. Emerging into the blaze of noon, she proved equal to the demands of public display and the management of men.

Worries about her successor declared themselves almost at once. Elizabeth was not particularly healthy, and she might well be assassinated. A successor might be needed at any time. Her counsellors dreaded the idea of an interregnum after her death – a time when rival claimants might decide to press their claims violently. There was another difficulty: with the death of the monarch all civil administration was halted, all offices vacated. If the successor was not proclaimed immediately, anarchy threatened. But Elizabeth was not even married. It seemed obvious that she must marry and produce an heir at once; but she declined to do so. She had many royal suitors (among them the Duke of Savoy, Erik XIV of Sweden, and last of all the French royal Duke of Alençon) and she got what political advantage she could from their courtships, but that was as far as it went. Given the right circumstances she might have married the Earl of Leicester, but she did not.

In fact, Elizabeth seems to have recoiled from the very idea of marrying. Her sometimes peremptory refusal to comply with the urgent promptings of Parliament and Council was a continual source of anxiety until she passed the age of childbearing, still unmarried. Thereafter, marriage would serve no purpose, and it was useless to continue the desperate coaxings, threats, and admonitions. Her advisers then made the best of a bad job and ensured that she was celebrated as the Virgin Queen, Gloriana, married only to her realm. An elaborate propagandist mythology was devised to suggest that her virginity was an entirely admirable and desirable state. Edmund Spenser was the great poet of this myth, but many others joined in, including Shakespeare, who made a passing allusion to it in *A*

Midsummer Night's Dream, when Puck describes Cupid taking aim

> At a fair vestal throned by the west...
> But I might see young Cupid's fiery shaft
> Quench'd in the chaste beams of the wat'ry moon,
> And the imperial vot'ress passed on
> In maiden meditation, fancy-free.
>
> (II.i.158–64)

Elizabeth herself never willingly discussed the matter, though she must have been aware of its importance.

When Elizabeth died in 1603, the Tudor dynasty, despite the various attempts to rescue it, came to its inevitable end, with the matter of the succession still in some doubt. She had kept silent about her successor, but seems to have accepted that it would be James Stuart, King of Scotland and son of her enemy Mary, Queen of Scots, by her marriage to the English Lord Darnley. Mary herself, while she lived, was probably the strongest claimant to Elizabeth's throne. She had been deposed in Scotland in favour of her infant son James, but had powerful foreign supporters. The decree by which the Pope sought to depose Elizabeth strengthened Mary's view that her cousin was a bastard and ineligible, and she had boldly displayed the royal arms of England. Her name was linked with various assassination plots, and Elizabeth, who never met Mary, saw to it that when she fled to England she spent years in prison. Eventually she was tried for treason and executed, after much procrastination on the part of the Queen.

Her son James, who had succeeded her in Scotland as James VI, was a descendant of Henry VII. He was interesting in his own way, pedantic, extravagant, and eccentric, 'the wisest fool

in Christendom', over-fond of handsome young men and theological disputation; he was not by any means a wholly satisfac-
tory monarch, but he was already a king, had been one since
infancy; and he was a father of sons. Himself the son of a
Catholic queen, he had endured in his youth the violence of
the Scottish nobility and the Scottish Reformation, and when
he came to England he tried hard to be irenic, to reconcile
the episcopate and the Puritans, as well as sponsoring the
so-called King James or Authorized translation of the Bible.
Unfortunately he quarrelled with his parliaments, as was to be
the way of his even more absolutist son Charles. Nevertheless,
he got off to a reasonable start. The last years of Elizabeth had
not been joyous – as she herself decayed, the nation suffered
bad harvests and inflation – and in 1603 James was given a
grand welcome in London.

It was an occasion of which, for once, it is right to say that it
began a new era, and, at least at first, it was understood to be
that. The Jacobean years were relatively peaceful and prosper-
ous, but it was not long before many were looking back nostal-
gically to the lost delights of Elizabeth's reign. Unlike his
predecessor, James feared city crowds and shunned public
appearances; worse, he brought large numbers of unwelcome
Scotsmen to London. He had favourites, he sold honours such
as baronetcies, which he more or less invented, and he spent
too much time hunting.

Elizabeth was remembered as more prudent and more
readily available to the people. Her Accession Day holiday (a
secular holiday instead of the old religious ones) continued to
be celebrated with masques and tilts while James's was not,
and indeed went on being celebrated in Westminster and
Merchant Taylors', great London schools, into the nineteenth

century. The old Queen once more became the focus of a cult not altogether remote from that of the Blessed Virgin. Sentimental veneration for her is reflected in Cranmer's speech in the *Henry VIII* of Shakespeare and Fletcher, dated 1613, a decade into the new reign. Cranmer speaks at the baptism of Elizabeth:

> In her days every man shall eat in safety
> Under his own vine what he plants, and sing
> The merry songs of peace to all his neighbours.
> God shall be truly known, and those about her
> From her shall read the perfect ways of honour,
> And by those claim their greatness, not by blood.
>
> (V.iv.32–7)

Cranmer goes on rather quickly to say equally fine things about James; but it is in the reign of Elizabeth rather than that of James that England has been thought of as merry.

Such, in short, were the problems associated with the Tudor succession. Two years after the Queen's death the great lawyer Francis Bacon remarked that the time of her reign and those of Edward and Mary provided 'the strangest variety that in a number of successions of any hereditary monarchy hath ever been known: the reign of a child, the offer of a usurpation, the reign of a lady married to a foreign prince, and the reign of a lady solitary and unmarried'. He had in mind Edward, Lady Jane Grey, Mary and Elizabeth. The Stuarts were to have their own succession difficulties; but that was later on.

Except in the matter of producing an heir, Elizabeth, who sur-
passed Deborah's forty years, was a success. During her long
reign she dealt with many obstinate problems of policy,
domestic and foreign. In an effort to restore national finances
she severely reduced Mary's expenditures, was reluctant to add
to the ranks of the nobility, and got rid of dukes; the last of
them, the Duke of Norfolk, who plotted against her, was
beheaded in 1572. She enjoyed plays and loved dancing and
other entertainments, but as far as possible ensured that the
cost would fall on her noble courtiers – her progresses and her
sojourns at their houses often cost them enormous sums.

On the other side of the account, she indulged favourites –
the Earl of Leicester, Sir Christopher Hatton, Sir Walter
Raleigh, and last, most disastrously, the Earl of Essex – and she
dispensed monopolies. These conferred fortunes on the lucky
recipients, who pocketed part of the profits on the commodi-
ties assigned to them; Raleigh, for instance, possessed monopolies on tin, playing cards, and tavern licences. Some
monopolies extended to foreign ports, and the beneficiaries
might grow rich by foreign trade without personal effort.

Yet despite her failings the Queen presided over an enormous national expansion and the beginnings of an overseas
empire. It was in her reign that the joint-stock company took
off. The Virginia Company was a lively concern, interested in

the tobacco trade at a time when tobacco was newly fashionable. The young John Donne unsuccessfully applied for a secretarial job in Virginia, and similar attempts must have been made by other young gentlemen from the Inns of Court. The East India Company, which in the course of time was to become the virtual ruler of India, made a profit of eighty-seven per cent on its first voyage, whereupon new shareholders hastened to subscribe more than a million pounds. There was even a Muscovy Company, trading with Russia.

Capital was now easily available for what Antonio, in *The Merchant of Venice*, called 'ventures', sharply distinguished from usury, which was what Shylock went in for. One sees that the apparent loss of Antonio's ships in *The Merchant of Venice* was a serious matter, at least in terms of the play, which ignores the fact that any merchant of Venice from the fourteenth century on would have been covered by insurance. Shylock was a moneylender, and it was traditional to frown on the usury business, though it was permitted within prescribed levels of interest, often breached. No doubt in the real world Shylock would have been an investor in the flourishing corporations, or in the insurance business. But the Antonio–Shylock plot does not belong to the actual world; it is a romance or a moral fable, like the story of the Three Caskets in the same play.

Commercially, London was catching up with Venice and the ports of the Netherlands. Foreign travel became more commonplace, merchant ships with valuable cargoes needed naval protection, and relations with Spain were such that it was patriotic to commit piracy at the enemy's expense. Drake's voyage in the *Golden Hind* made fantastic profits for those who invested in it; the Queen is said to have spent her share on reducing the national debt and offering extravagant entertainments to her last suitor, the French royal Duke of Alençon.

London, as an increasingly important centre of commerce and capital, changed enormously during Elizabeth's reign. New money was everywhere in evidence. Great quantities of meat were consumed, glass was replacing pewter, clothes were both elaborate and expensive. The streets were crowded and quarrelsome; men carried swords, and a recent addition to street weaponry was the dag, or pistol. The actors, at home in the demi-monde, played their part in street crime; Ben Jonson, for instance, killed the actor Gabriel Spencer in an unlawful duel with rapiers, and Spencer himself had killed James Feake, the son of a goldsmith, in a brawl in Shoreditch. The expensive drug of choice was tobacco, smoked in clay pipes and sold, along with bottled ale, at the theatres; a pipeful cost three-pence, three times as much as going to the theatre. Tobacco smoking was much hated by James I, who wrote against the habit in his *Counter-blast to Tobacco* (1604); some of his condemnations will remind the reader of more recent history:

And for the vanities committed in this filthy custom, is it not great vanity and uncleanness, that at the table, a place of respect, of cleanliness, of modesty, men should not be ashamed to sit tossing of tobacco pipes, and puffing of the smoke of tobacco one to another, making the filthy smoke and stink thereof to exhale athwart the dishes, and infect the air, when very often men that abhor it are at their repast? Surely smoke becomes a kitchen far better than a dining chamber, and yet it makes a kitchen also oftentimes in the inward parts of men, soiling and infecting them with an unctuous and oily kind of soot, as hath been found in some great tobacco takers, that after their death were opened.

We may suppose that the theatres, though large and grand, being the haunt of apprentices and law students as well as more splendid persons, were noisy and smelly and often the scene of quarrels, like the adjacent inns and whorehouses. They were literally adjacent: the Rose Theatre, hard by the Globe, was built in the grounds of a brothel. All around were card-sharps and dicers, con men and moneylenders, roaring boys and roaring girls. The actors were identified by their enemies with this rabble; as one critical observer remarked:

> For a man to put on woman's apparel, and a woman a man's, is plain prohibition; I speak not of execrable oaths, artificial lies, discoveries of cozenage, scurrilous words, obscene discourses, licentious motions, lascivious actions, and lewd gestures; for all these are incident to other men. But here is the difference: in these they come by imperfection, in them by profession.

The most delightful picture of London as a paradise of rogues and cheats is Ben Jonson's comedy *The Alchemist*, performed at the Globe by Shakespeare's company, the King's Men, in 1610. But tales of 'conny-catching' – duping the simple-minded – abound in the literature of the period. The venal manners of the merchant class are treated in the city comedies of Middleton and others. Of the delinquencies and corruptions of Shakespeare's time we have ample information, as no doubt he had.

It was into this turbulent city that William Shakespeare made his way as a young man, frequenting, as he must, the parts of London and Southwark that eluded the attentions of the Puritan city fathers. By what means he came there, and exactly what he did when he got there, are still questions with no clear answers. Some conjectures now in fashion require us to believe that the poet was, or had been, Catholic, and that his Catholic faith was one reason why he found himself working in the London theatre.

Adherents of the old faith tended to occur in geographical pockets – Warwickshire was one such, and Lancashire another, and a sojourn in Lancashire forms part of Shakespeare's conjectural early career. His father was born in 1529 when everybody was a Catholic, though Henry VIII was already in dispute with the papacy. John Shakespeare lived through the reigns of Edward and Mary and almost to the end of Elizabeth's, dying in 1601. It can be said that he witnessed all the tidal changes in Tudor ecclesiastical history, and he could very well have been one of those who felt some measure of allegiance to the old faith, which he might have recommended to his children. A businessman of some substance, he was at various times alderman, High Bailiff, and Justice of the Peace. For some years he kept the accounts of the small market town of Stratford, and he did so under the aegis of the pre-Reformation Holy Cross

Guild. But later he fell on hard times, his business troubles compounded, it seems, by his recusancy – failing to go to church as the law insisted everybody must. Perhaps, as he claimed, he was avoiding his creditors, but it could have been his conscience that kept him at home. Certainly he was fined for staying away from church.

In 1757 there was found in the rafters of John Shakespeare's house in Stratford a document known as his Spiritual Last Will and Testament. Unfortunately the document has been lost, but it is known to have been a translation of Cardinal Borromeo's 'Last Will of the Soul', written in the 1570s and now made his own by John Shakespeare. Copies of this profession of Catholic Counter-Reformation faith apparently circulated all over Europe. The English Jesuit missionary and martyr Edmund Campion had visited Borromeo in 1580 and is known to have brought many copies, perhaps thousands, of this document in English translation for distribution to the persecuted faithful in England. John Shakespeare seems to have acknowledged possession of his copy, perhaps by adding his mark in lieu of signature, but the document, once in the hands of the late-eighteenth-century Shakespearian pioneer Edmond Malone (who came to doubt its authenticity), unfortunately disappeared.

On this lost document, along with some other rather shaky testimonies, rests a theory now thriving among literary historians. Campion is known to have passed close to Stratford on his way to Lancashire in 1580, no doubt distributing copies of Borromeo's pamphlet to Catholics, including, conceivably, John Shakespeare. Government measures against the missionaries were at this time as harsh as can be imagined, and Campion would have had to be careful about the people he trusted. If the older Shakespeare was one such person, would not the priest also meet his son, the sixteen-year-old William? Some resist these speculations, pointing out that John Shakespeare, as an important Stratford official, must have had a hand in the Protestant defacement of local churches, but there is evidence, including the fine for recusancy, on the other side. It is even suggested that Campion took the young William with him when he went on his way to Lancashire.

There exists a tradition, started or endorsed by John Aubrey (1626–97) in his variably dependable *Brief Lives*, that as a young man Shakespeare worked as a schoolmaster 'in the country'. It is believed by some that the allusion is to the poet's having had his first job in Lancashire, in the family of Alexander Hoghton, whose will, made in 1581, when Shakespeare was seventeen, asks that his neighbour Thomas Hesketh either take 'William Shakeshafte' into his service or find him 'some good master'. Shakeshafte was also left a year's wages and an annuity of £2. The assumption is that Shakeshafte was Shakespeare. In Hoghton's service he could have worked as a tutor and also as an actor, for this wealthy Catholic family cultivated the drama. The Hoghton house was just the sort of place to hide a priest, and the servants, including Shakeshafte, would be certified good Catholics. Since Campion himself was in the house at approximately the right time, he might have used his theatrical experience, gained during his five years at the university in Prague, to teach the young fellow the elements of his craft. But the execution of Campion and the death of Hoghton in 1581 made it impossible for the student actor to remain in Lancashire, so he returned to Stratford, where, under his own name and still legally a minor, he married Anne Hathaway near the end of 1582.

Meanwhile Hesketh – so the Shakeshafte tale continues –

honoured his obligation under his friend's will and got Shakespeare into the service of Lord Derby, the Lancashire magnate, and his son Lord Strange, who kept a professional company of players. So the young man found himself not in Lancashire, and not in the Jesuit College at Douai, as Campion might have hoped, but in London, where he was to make his mark on a more innocent scaffold than those which staged the gruesome deaths of the Jesuit martyrs. Even so, he was a bold young fellow: he might just have stayed in Stratford, spent time with his family, and exploited a gift for business dealing that could have given him all the civic honours his father accumulated, and more. But he chose the theatre and a different kind of celebrity.

It will perhaps be noticed that these speculations grow more and more far-fetched as one 'might have' succeeds another, or a 'may well have' or a 'surely'. A principal reason for their popularity may be the long-felt irritation of Shakespearians that the biography of Shakespeare should contain a blank period known as 'the lost years'. These are the years between the last record of his living in Stratford – his presumable presence in February 1585 at the christening of his twins Hamnet and Judith – and the first mention of him as known to literary and dramatic circles in London. This was Robert Greene's sneer at him in his *Groatsworth of Wit Worth a Million of Repentance*, written in 1592, as a 'Shake-scene', an 'upstart crow beautified with our feathers' (a phrase endlessly reinterpreted, but certainly not friendly, and perhaps envious; it does show that the young man was already eminent enough to attract hostility from a senior playwright).

A second motive is to strengthen the argument that Shakespeare was a Catholic. One defender of this view ends his essay on 'Religion in Arden' thus: 'Surely...from the depths of his heart Shakespeare looks fondly back to the time before far-reaching changes had been inaugurated by Henry VIII and ratified by his daughter Elizabeth'. Sentimentality has always been a nuisance in Shakespeare studies. Of course Shakespeare, like his father and his father's generation (and like most fathers in most generations), may have looked back with some regret to the old days without feeling obliged to offer strong resistance to change, and in so doing to defy the law. Admittedly Catholics might have had a keener sense of what had been forfeited to Reform; John Shakespeare may, after all, have returned to the old faith. And there were conversions to Catholicism, Ben Jonson's among them. But there is no evidence that Shakespeare chose that way. Had he been, as some claim, a lifelong Catholic, it is strange that no unequivocal trace of his beliefs can be found in his thirty-seven plays. Moreover, the case for Shakespeare as a Protestant has sturdy defenders. David Daniell mentions a surviving copy of the Second Folio (1632) that was censored by the Inquisition. The censor 'found much to delete'; yet he rather surprisingly spared *King John*, a frankly anti-papistical play, and bafflingly cut the whole of *Measure for Measure*. Was this because of the Duke's unsatisfactory performance as a friar in disguise, or because this bogus friar reveals the secrets of the confessional?

Daniell concludes with due moderation that the entire *oeuvre* of Shakespeare provides no evidence as to his religious adherence – a conclusion too dull for the Shakeshaftians. It does, however, appear that he used the Great Bible of 1539, which is reflected in the scriptural texts quoted in the *Book of Common Prayer*, a likely source; and that at least in his later career he also used the Geneva Bible (1560), with all the

33

Calvinist marginalia that had such an influence on the development of doctrine in the Protestant English church. Of course, to use the Geneva Bible need not imply a complete loss of interest in the old faith; it is perfectly plausible that Shakespeare and many non-Catholic or ex-Catholic contemporaries used it, yet retained an interest in Purgatory. Purgatory had been a dominant idea and much argued over: what was the character of the torments? How many persons suffered in it, and for how long? How big was it (horribly small for such numbers)? Do the prayers of a bereaved family shorten one's time in it? It might be hard to lose all interest in such matters.

Hamlet, who hadn't, went to college not at Douai but at Wittenberg, the university of Luther and Melanchthon, and the centre of the continental Reformation. Is that a clue? But Wittenberg happened to be the university favoured by Danes studying abroad (from 1586 to 1595 it had on its rolls two students named Rosenkrantz and Gyldenstjerne). Wittenberg was described by an English writer in 1600 as a 'learned seminary of the arts'; these would certainly include the arts of discourse, and may or may not have involved polemical theology. The best, though no doubt the dullest, answer may be that any intelligent contemporary of Hamlet and of Shakespeare would be familiar with both sides of the case and might be reluctant to organize their religious sentiments, as the clergy were forced to do, in terms of doctrines and prohibitions handed down from the new Supreme Governors of the Church and their theologians.

Incidentally, those who want to believe in the poet's Catholicism and his formative sojourn in Lancashire seem to put too much weight on the name 'Shakeshafte', a claim for the identity of this boy with the Stratford Shakespeare which may be thought to invite a sceptical response. That form of the name is said to have been recorded in Lancashire at the time, and it is sometimes hinted that the young man adopted it as a disguise. But this is extremely unlikely. Why would the change of name (hardly even a change, if 'Shakeshafte' was a variant of the same name) make this obscure youth any more secure? And if he chose to take a new name for reasons of security, why would he choose so transparent an alias? As for the rest of the story, it may be thought a fiction, one bright idea breeding from another, the whole dependent on a prior aspiration to get Shakespeare from Stratford to London via Lancashire with Lord Strange's Men, and to close the gap between the Stratford baptismal record and the bitter recognition given him by Robert Greene's attack in 1592. The older story of his joining a travelling troupe at Stratford is also mere conjecture, but it serves as well to get the young man to London, and it sets at rest the anxieties of all who cannot bear to think of Shakespeare's having had quite a long spell of life that remains completely private, of which they know nothing. However, it lacks the conspiratorial detail that makes the rival theory more attractive.

In the absence of evidence one might be tempted to offer one's own rival explanation: perhaps Shakespeare went to London not as an actor and not with theatrical ambitions, but as a poet seeking a patron, having somehow got wind of one. Somehow he found Southampton, and his most elaborate early works, *Venus and Adonis* and *The Rape of Lucrece* (1593 and 1594), are dedicated to that earl. Alone among his publications these works are carefully printed and proofed, as if he might have regarded them as belonging to his true career. He seems to have been on respectfully familiar terms with Southampton, a leading courtier and disciple of Essex. The dedication to *Venus and Adonis* ('the first heir of my invention', which shows he wasn't counting the early plays among his achievements, or the achievements he would confess to in these circles) was preceded by a Latin motto meaning that while others concern themselves with base matters, he will try for a purer poetry, which, he flatteringly implies, patronage alone makes possible. A year later the dedication to *The Rape of Lucrece* is unusually warm, suggesting that there had been, in the interval between the two poems, some increase in the intimacy of patron and poet. It could well be that Shakespeare's first ambition was to be a page-poet rather than a stage-poet.

As is well known, these long works were written during a protracted closure of the theatres because of the plague, and while his fellow actors travelled the country, Shakespeare seems to have abandoned them to their provincial fate and stayed in London writing poems. But before he wrote them Shakespeare had produced the *Henry VI* plays and possibly other works (*Titus Andronicus, The Comedy of Errors* and doubtless more), so it is argued that the poems were written only because there was at the time no call for plays. But a poet might well, without thinking of it as a career choice, have turned to the theatre to make a living, much as young poets and novelists nowadays turn their hands to newspaper reviewing as a way of supporting themselves. Short of cash, one might be eager to join one of Philip Henslowe's playwright teams, with up to five men working on one play and payment 'in the hand'. In fact many of the writers we think of first as dramatists were poets in a more dignified sense. Ben Jonson was one, who wrote collaboratively as well as individually for the stage ('the loathed stage', as he called it), and yet was probably the most distinguished lyric poet of the age. Lesser figures –

Greene, Nashe, Marston, Dekker and many others – wrote in many genres as well as in the dramatic. However, it must be admitted that Shakespeare, when enabled – perhaps by a gift or loan from Southampton – to acquire a share in the Lord Chamberlain's Men and the Globe, seems to have given up the 'purer' forms of poetry and written little except plays. Perhaps keeping up with the demands of his theatrical colleagues was as much as he could do. However, at some time or other he wrote the Sonnets, probably in the 1590s when he normally did have other work to do.

We do not come close to knowing about Shakespeare's early London years in detail, but we can take it for granted that the capital was a shock after Stratford. The conditions of life in this metropolitan city have been sketched above. The population of the whole country was between three and four million, and only during the reign of Elizabeth had it returned to the level it had reached before the Black Death a century earlier. London was by far the most populous city, with up to half a million inhabitants. Its nearest rivals were ports like Bristol, Dover and Southampton, or major regional centres, of which the richest was Norwich, centre of the wool trade that built the great churches of East Anglia. The recently incorporated borough of Stratford was a small town of about one thousand inhabitants, tiny compared with London; but such small centres were important for their markets and courts of justice.

Accustomed as we have become to fast trains and roads, we need an effort of imagination to understand how slow travel must have been on roads that were always bad and often impassable in winter. Stratford was at least a two-day horseback ride or a four-day walk from London. It would have been difficult to foster any strong sense of nationality – as opposed to regionality, or local patriotism – had not the church and Crown provided some common ground. One of the changes wrought by Elizabeth was to make something more akin to modern patriotism a substitute for the old religious tokens and bonds, the liturgical celebrations and the guilds. The Tudor grammar schools with their more or less uniform curricula may also have established the possibility of loyalty to a community of the educated laity. We must assume Shakespeare, as the son of a prominent citizen, to have attended Stratford's Guild School. The existence of such establishments ensured that Latin did not belong solely to priest and lawyer. Rhetoric was taught less as a vocational than as a cultural acquirement, a means to self-fulfilment. Since all the textbooks, including those we may assume the young Shakespeare to have worked through, derived from the same sources, there was a measure of genuine uniformity in humanist education.

It was in this age that the book became a familiar object, with incalculable consequences. Since records are fairly thorough, it is known that between 1558 and 1579, 2760 books were published in London. Between 1580 and 1603 the number rose to 4370. John Guy calculates, on the basis of an average print run of 1250 copies, that 'this represents an average of just two books per head of a population of 4¼ million over a generation and a half'. Part of the endless bustle around St Paul's must have been caused by the bookstalls, for St Paul's, in a sense the social centre of the city, was also the centre of the book trade, and it was not far from where the newly arrived aspirant would find himself. The proportion of citizens who read may seem small, but there were enough of them to make bestsellers, one of which was Shakespeare's *Venus and Adonis*, an example of the fashionable Ovidian-erotic mode, which went into nine editions in the poet's lifetime. One could go to St Paul's and buy a sermon, or a sixpenny quarto of a play, or almost any other sort of book, from devotional tracts to romances.

For many centuries the Bible of the Catholic Church was the Vulgate, the Latin translation of St Jerome. The Church long resisted translations, but when they became available it was possible to study the groundwork of Christian faith in one's own tongue, translated not from a Latin translation but from the original Hebrew and Greek. *Sola scriptura:* Rome, said Luther, was no longer in control of interpretation; the Bible alone decided points of doctrine; and now interpretations could be in deadly conflict. The Geneva Bible, as one would expect, offered glosses animated by extreme Protestant conviction, and for the next fifty years it was the version most read in England. Interest in matters of theological interpretation, fostered by access to this primary source, were of spiritual importance, since they concerned the fate of the individual sinner; but they also encouraged close reading and an understanding of linguistic subtleties. Theological issues occur in Shakespeare's plays, and sometimes (as in *Measure for Measure*) he is dramatizing an ethical conflict arising from a Pauline text. But even when this is not evidently the case, we can be sure that a habit of scrupulous examination of difficult language was a part of his equipment quite as important as the humanist indoctrination in rhetoric undergone at school.

Living as he must have in this environment of books, and himself writing poems and plays, the young Shakespeare would be aware that books could be dangerous as well as instructive. From 1586 onwards, every title proposed for publication had to be licensed by the Archbishop of Canterbury or the Bishop of London – a pre-censorship distinct from that applying to plays, which had to be passed by the Master of the Revels in the office of the Lord Chamberlain and certified as 'allowed' before they were performed. In Book I of *The Faerie Queene*, Spenser represents Error as spewing out seditious pamphlets (I.i.172–80). The authorities, always anxious about public disorder of any kind, were keen to uncover hints of sedition in books as well as in other manifestations.

In this restless, always changing city, what sort of people would Shakespeare come into contact with? The inhabitants were of many kinds: country people came into the city to work or seek work, foreign refugees sought an occasionally precarious asylum, gentlemen from the universities came to complete their studies at the Inns of Court. Smaller civic communities were hierarchical in social structure – one might have to acknowledge subservience to a local grandee – but a certain neighbourliness was possible, and citizens largely ran their own affairs, so that a butcher or glover like Shakespeare's father could be quite an eminent figure in the community.

But change was occurring even in those circles; a new ruling class, enriched by monastic spoil or commercial success, was replacing the old nobility, its traditions of hospitality now in eclipse. There was litigation arising from the enclosures that were bringing to an end the old system of strip farming and common pasture, and a succession of bad harvests in the last decade of the century (mentioned in *A Midsummer Night's Dream* II.i.88–105) caused food shortages and popular unrest. Inflation was severe; the cost of living was multiplied three and a half times in the course of the century, and was certainly not under control in the time of James I. No one had any idea how to deal with this problem, and there were attempts to debase the coinage. Inflation bore hard on the urban journeyman, whose pay only doubled in the same period even though he was required to work longer hours with fewer holidays than in the Catholic past. But the rich were hardly affected, and many were building grand country houses with the proceeds of the dissolution of monastic properties. The merchant class also prospered, and so did courtiers favoured with monopolies.

Meanwhile the capital was transformed. A foreign visitor, Paul Hentzner, was astonished by its grandeur, admiring it as 'the seat of the British Empire' and commenting that 'the wealth of the world is wafted to it by the Thames'. (But let us remember that it was also used as a sewer, so that not only wealth was wafted by the Thames.) So the rich grew richer, their lives more luxurious and ostentatious, while the poor grew poorer. These were the early days of capitalism. Nature contributed further causes of infelicity: sexually transmitted diseases were rife, and the topic of many jokes in and out of plays; leprosy had virtually disappeared, but smallpox and malaria had not, and the greatest threat of all was bubonic plague, its visitations frequent and sometimes prolonged. Its causes were not understood, though the authorities were well aware that places where crowds gathered – for instance, in theatres – must be closed when the death toll rose beyond a certain point. Along with the fear of foreign Catholic enemies, such were the main anxieties of the time.

Yet the social structure still stood, and it was possible, as Sir Thomas Smith expressed it in his book *De Republica Anglorum* (roughly translated, 'concerning the political arrangements of the English', 1583), to 'divide our men into four sorts: gentlemen, citizens or burgesses, yeomen artificers, and labourers'. Shakespeare's father was a burgess, and later, when his son procured a grant of arms for him, a gentleman.

Ben Jonson made fun of Shakespeare for sporting the new coat of arms – it was at the time an unusual promotion for a theatrical person, though it became more common as the profession prospered. In later years it was equally unusual for a professional dramatist like Jonson to publish his *Works* just as if he were a gentleman writer, and he was ridiculed for it in his turn. These are signs of what later came to be called upward mobility, traceable in a profession whose members had fairly recently been treated as vagabonds and vagrants. Shakespeare himself has some wry remarks on acquired gentility in *The Winter's Tale*, when the shepherds who found Perdita and the treasure that accompanied her declare themselves 'gentlemen born', claiming to have been so 'any time these four hours' (V.ii.135–6).

One should add to Smith's list another class, or underclass, growing, in these years, ever larger and more difficult to handle, namely 'masterless men', who worked the London streets or were unwelcome wanderers, liable to be whipped, from parish to parish. The Poor Laws, though to some extent softened in the Queen's later years, remained severe. The penalties of ear-boring and death for vagrancy were given up, and some provision was made to award pensions to wounded soldiers and sailors, but an act of 1598 nevertheless provided sentences of whipping, prison or the galleys for bad characters. (Only a couple of years before the passing of this act, Falstaff remarked after the battle of Shrewsbury that his conscripts would be left in their battered state at the town's end 'to beg during life' (*1 Henry IV* V.iii.39).

So Shakespeare arrived in town, and somehow made the acquaintance of a patron, Henry Wriothesley, third Earl of Southampton, in the view of many not only the dedicatee of the poems but the young man of the Sonnets, perhaps both lover and rival in love. Southampton was of the party of Essex, stepson of the Earl of Leicester, who had meant much to Elizabeth; and Essex, in his turn, was the Queen's favourite in her later years, though the relationship was difficult and ended in disaster with the execution of Essex and the imprisonment of Southampton. Essex gets a notable mention in the Chorus to Act V of *Henry V*, written while he was supposed to be quelling revolt in Ireland; the Chorus hopes he will return 'bringing rebellion broached on his sword' (l. 32). In fact he returned in disgrace. It seems likely that Shakespeare had him momentarily in mind some years later when he wrote *Coriolanus*, a study of a heroic but intemperate aristocrat; the comparison of this tragic figure with Essex was not new.

Essex was in his day powerful but arrogant, a hot defender of the rights of the aristocracy and, along with the lawyer and philosopher Francis Bacon, an opponent of the Queen's first minister, Robert Cecil. Despite her generous treatment of him, Essex quarrelled dangerously with the Queen and plotted against her, a development that gave rise to what is probably the most celebrated moment of Shakespeare's connection with the Essex faction.

In 1601, on the eve of Essex's fatal rebellion, a certain Gelly Meyrick, an officer of Essex's household, commissioned from Shakespeare's company a special performance of *Richard II*, a play about Richard's deposition by Henry Bolingbroke, later Henry IV. The idea seems to have been to win the crowd over to Essex's cause. The actors protested that the play was old and 'long out of use' (it was probably first performed in 1595), but they accepted a fee of £2 and did as Meyrick had requested. The play was well known and had been in print since 1597, though without the scene enacting the actual deposition. The players rarely condoned the printing of their plays while they were still attracting audiences, but two more editions appeared, with a fourth in 1608, this time including the deposition scene. It is not known whether that scene was included in the command performance, but it survived into the next reign, and the censor – the same man who had forbidden it during Elizabeth's reign – cannot have thought it dangerous to James, for he allowed it to be printed.

Essex, in disgrace because of his conduct in Ireland, was under house arrest. On the day after the Globe performance he broke out and led his followers into the city, where he sought to rally the citizenry of London to his cause, which was probably to oust the ageing Queen. The attempt failed disastrously; Essex was arrested for treason on 19 February and beheaded on the twenty-fifth, less than two weeks after the special performance of Shakespeare's play.

It might be thought that the actors took a foolish risk in accepting this commission, particularly since Sir John Hayward was at that very moment under interrogation for a book published in 1599 that treated of the misdeeds of Richard. And he had dedicated the book to Essex. Committed to the

Tower, Hayward denied that he had intended parallels between Richard and Elizabeth, but he could not satisfy her and remained in prison until she died. Yet Shakespeare's company got away almost scot-free. Possibly the reason for their escape was that they were mere actors, unlike Sir Gelly Meyrick, who was executed like his leader; or it may be that their protector Lord Hunsdon could argue that they performed under duress, Essex being so mighty a lord.

Elizabeth is known to have resented comparisons between her and Richard, who was notorious for his absolutist pretensions and his dependence on favourites. 'I am Richard II, know ye not that?' she asked the antiquary William Lambarde, her Keeper of the Rolls, complaining that the play had been performed 'above forty times in open streets and houses'. She was by this stage in her life irascible and disordered, but here she may just have been flippant. 'Forty' need not be taken to mean more than 'many' times. Lambarde made a tactful reply: 'Such a wicked imagination was determined and attempted by a most unkind gentleman, the most adorned creature that ever your majesty made.' This remark is less interesting as a model of how to converse with a dangerous woman than for its use of the word 'imagination', of which it is easy to miss the sinister undertones. The word was juridically associated with treasonable plotting, or even with just thinking about such plotting, against the monarch's life. It could refer to an intention to harm him or her 'without an actual effect of it', and it was a capital offence. It was used in this sense at the trial of the regicides in 1660 (*OED* v. 2). John Barrell, in his book *Imagining the King's Death* (2000), shows that the concept was still operative at treason trials in the late eighteenth century. This usage of 'imagination' may sound peculiar, but we should recognize it as employed in this sense when Antonio in *The Tempest* (II.i.208–9), plotting against Alonso, says 'My strong imagination sees a crown / Dropping upon thy head.' In these years, long before Coleridge had drastically elevated its meaning, treason and murder lurked in the word 'imagination'. Lambarde was a scholar, and so was the Queen. He needed to make his point strongly; she responded in kind, lamenting the ingratitude of all (not just one) who, despite all the favours she had shown them, insisted on doing plays about Richard II. Lambarde died shortly after this perhaps rather exacting interview.

It tends to be forgotten, when this tale is told, that the Lambarde conversation took place on 4 August 1601, six months after the execution of Essex. There was no more danger from that quarter, and after that lapse of time we should not assume that the Queen was referring to the one-time performance of early February. Anyway, the actors, unlike Hayward, got away with it and were sufficiently in favour to be asked to perform at court on the eve of Essex's execution. Perhaps Augustine Phillips, the actor who spoke for the company at the inquiry, managed to convince his interrogators that they really hadn't wanted to put the play on. The quality of mercy did not figure largely in the conduct of Elizabethan grandees, and it sounds as if on this occasion at least they thought the behaviour of the actors not all that important, even though it was associated with Essex, who was on trial for treason. Perhaps the connection between plays and contemporary politics was less close and important than is sometimes alleged. Writers in quest of connections and significances sometimes misread or ignore evidence. In December 1597, Sir Edward Hoby invited Robert Cecil to his house to see 'K. Richard present himself',

presumably in a play, possibly Shakespeare's, possibly somebody else's. (And of course he may just have meant *Richard
III*.) In any case, Cecil was the most powerful of ministers and
a sworn enemy of Essex. If the play in question was in fact
about Richard II, are we to imagine that Cecil had it in mind to
be critical of his Queen?

The whole story raises the question whether it can be right,
as many now claim, to see the theatres of 1601 and later as
having acquired great political relevance and power. As we
have seen, the companies existed only by virtue of their
courtly protectors, in Shakespeare's case the Lord
Chamberlain, and from 1603 the new king. When they seemed
to be growing too dangerous they were closed down, not by the
court of Charles I, which had left London, but by the now
Puritan Parliament, always the enemy of the theatre but now
having the excuse that 'public sports do not well agree with
public calamities, nor public stage-plays with the Seasons of
Humiliation'. From time to time members of the companies
got into various scrapes – Ben Jonson was accused of sedition
for his part in the lost play *The Isle of Dogs*, but after a few
weeks in prison he continued his career. Marlowe was murdered, but that was when he was apparently engaged in his
second career as a spy. But we could surely not attribute to
either of them, or to any of their colleagues, including the
apparently blameless Shakespeare, the imagination of treason.

We may conclude that the connection between Shakespeare's
company and the court was important, at least to the players,
but hardly intimate. What was his professional standing in the
early London years? We know from Greene's attack on him as
'the only Shake-scene in the country' that he had made some
sort of mark by 1592. There is no end to arguments about the

chronology of the early plays, but we can believe that by the time of Greene's complaint Shakespeare had produced, or collaborated in, three *Henry VI* plays and perhaps others; the Oxford editors, after studying the evidence and conducting all manner of tests, would add *The Two Gentlemen of Verona* (1590–1), *The Taming of the Shrew* (1590–1), *Titus Andronicus* (1592), and possibly the very successful *Richard III*, which combined with the three parts of *Henry VI* to form the earlier of the two historical tetralogies.

Of the other companies working at the time, the most important was the Queen's Men, formed in 1583, into which the best actors, including the celebrated comic Richard Tarleton, had been drafted. At this time the best-known playwright was John Lyly, who wrote courtly comedies for boys' companies. But there were several other adult companies; Shakespeare's plays at this time seem to have been performed by the Lord Strange's Men. Actors apparently moved quite often from one to another, and sometimes companies merged. What looks like a confused state of affairs ended when the plague closed the theatres in 1593. When they reopened in 1594 there was a major rearrangement, as a result of which Shakespeare became a sharer in what was thenceforth the most important company, the Lord Chamberlain's Men (after 1603 the King's Men), with whom he remained for the rest of his career. The chief rival company was now the Admiral's Men, with the great actor Edward Alleyn (a son-in-law of Henslowe's) as the star.

So, from the age of thirty, Shakespeare was to have the protection of the Lord Chamberlain, a connection of great value. As we have seen, the City fathers did not approve of theatres, fearing public disorder and the spread of disease; without courtly support the theatres could not have survived. The trick was to pretend that the public performances of the protected companies were merely rehearsals for their court appearances, which were frequent. As Dominic Baker-Smith remarks, 'the court was, in effect, the guaranty of the theatre in its most creative period; and the break in dramatic history heralded by the closure of the theatres in 1642 as the court quit London tells its own story.' Meanwhile Southampton, a more private courtly contact, dropped out of the picture. Those who believe he was the young man of the Sonnets can argue that it was the quarrel over the Dark Lady that brought his friendship with Shakespeare to an end. But although there seems to have been a relationship of sorts, it is unlikely to have been other than deferential on the poet's side (and of course it is not a certainty that Southampton had any part in the Sonnets). As previously remarked, serious poetry was almost completely dependent on the fickle favour of patrons; we know how Edmund Spenser, a far greater name than Shakespeare and the master poet of the age, had to defer to his distant relations, the Spencers of Althorp, as well as to other great men like Leicester and Essex; and he was entitled to complain about the stinginess of the Queen to the celebration of whose glories he had devoted so much of his life.

In the early days of Shakespeare's company, its prime interest was in the public theatres, large open-air structures like the Theatre and then the Globe, which was, as it were, born of it. Later the company was to develop a profitable interest in the private or indoor theatre (indeed, it bought part of the Blackfriars precinct in 1596, but the wealthy inhabitants of the neighbourhood prevented them for a dozen years from using it as a theatre). The lease on their public playhouse, the Theatre, expired in 1597, and for two years before that, the company, involved in a wrangle with the landlord, had not been able to use it. Having invested heavily in the unusable Blackfriars, they were for a time in financial straits, but they solved their problem with a remarkable coup. They rented a site on Bankside, surreptitiously dismantled the Theatre, carried its timbers across the Thames, and used them in the construction of the Globe in 1598.

By this time Shakespeare had emerged as the leading playwright of the company, and perhaps of London generally. His way to this eminence had been cleared by the early death of Christopher Marlowe, killed in a tavern brawl in 1593; and, once achieved, it was not challenged in the years before his apparent retirement or semi-retirement in 1611. The company performed more often than others at court. Under the jurisdiction of the Lord Chamberlain, its sponsor, the Master of the

Revels, Edmund Tilney, chose the plays for court performance, as well as censoring them. He also licensed the theatres. He seems to have done well out of the fees he charged (seven shillings per play examined), with other benefits, such as the house that went with the job, which he kept from 1579 till his death in 1610.

The company's relations with Tilney and his deputy, George Buck (who increased the reading fee to £1), lasted throughout Shakespeare's career, and were on the whole peaceful. Yet the office had considerable punitive power, for Tilney's commission gave him a duty 'to warn, command, and appoint in all places within this our realm of England, as well within franchises and liberties as without, all and every player or players, with their playmakers, either belonging to any nobleman, or otherwise, bearing the name or names or using the faculty of playmakers, or players of comedies, tragedies, interludes, or what other shows soever, from time to time and at all times, to appear before him with all such plays, tragedies, comedies, or shows, as they shall have in readiness, or mean to set forth...' And so on. Tilney had the right to lock up offenders until he deemed the punishment sufficient.

This was certainly censorship; and on occasion official powers were exercised. The manuscript of the play of *Sir Thomas More*, written by several hands including Shakespeare's, was rejected because of its depiction of public disorder, and even though the part Shakespeare wrote was a condemnation of such disorder, the play was not performed. Jonson and his collaborators Chapman and Marston ran into trouble with their play *Eastward Ho!* (1605), which was satirical about the King and the court, and the boys' company that played it at Blackfriars (the Children of the Revels) got into more scrapes. Though it does not seem that Tilney was very severe, nevertheless the threat was always there, and it is unlikely that many plays that could be thought seditious or otherwise objectionable would have been submitted to his office. The Master of the Revels was the Company's defender against its main enemies, the City authorities, and they would not want to make an enemy of him.

By the late 1590s the London theatre was well established and the trades of playmaking and acting well developed. The distance between the earlier drama – the miracle and morality plays, the performances of travelling actors and acrobats – and the work of the professional London stage was by now great. Yet in a sense there was real continuity between the old and the new. Even when the Globe was in its heyday the company was occasionally forced to tour, sometimes in Europe. The elements of simple display – the sword-fighting, the droll and often slightly obscene playlet called the 'jig' at the end of the main performance – were valued survivals. Theatrical display was also continuous with the manifestations of civic and royal pomp. The Lord Mayor's Show was a great annual ceremony, and the Queen had, on occasion, to give what was in effect a royal performance. 'We princes,' she remarked, 'are set on stage in the sight and view of the whole world.' The traditionally elaborate Christmas celebrations gave scope to the comic invention of the Lords of Misrule appointed at the Inns of Court. Even the ghastly ceremonies that accompanied executions at Tyburn and elsewhere had a theatrical quality. The theatre in Shakespeare's time was certainly a business, and its products no longer very like the plays put on by the Coventry guilds, but the business was made possible by a continuing liking and aptitude for drama, for colour, excitement, and fine speech.

The boys' companies, sometimes serious rivals to the adults – a matter Hamlet discusses with Rosencrantz and Guildenstern in the Folio version of *Hamlet* (II.ii.338ff.) – belonged to a more academic tradition and, since they played indoors, appealed to a more refined audience (an advantage later cancelled by the adults when they acquired indoor theatres). Probably their acting styles were different; the boys did not need to command large audiences in a big space. And one would expect much greater powers of development in a company with a permanent body of adult performers; the boys' brief careers ended when they were still immature and doubtless under instruction by teachers, themselves not necessarily actors. Many years of playing must have given Burbage and his companions greater resources, more 'tonal variety', to borrow an expression of Peter Thomson's. The skills of a Burbage were what enabled Shakespeare to create complex characters – the power of 'personation', a word that, along with 'personate', seems to have come into use at this time, and is first found in John Florio's Italian dictionary, *A World of Words* (1598). Shakespeare probably knew Florio, who was Southampton's secretary and, as a keen theatregoer, may have picked up the word in theatrical circles. It is tempting to think that it was a new refinement in acting style, facilitated by and encouraging a new flexibility in dramatic verse, that made this word necessary.

The increased variety of dramatic blank verse, the principal medium of all the plays, supports the view that its development, and the development of acting, came on together. No longer so restricted by their rhetorical training, the adult actors must have developed a much freer style. They were, at any rate to a great extent, liberated from the old rant and the old systems of gesture that accompanied rhetorical delivery. This is what Hamlet is talking about when he offers his advice to the actors (II.ii). Shakespeare more than once demonstrated quite deliberately the distance between the new and the old manners.

Andrew Gurr notes a growing distinction between *acting* and *playing*, the first term progressively applied only to the professionals. 'Action', once the term for the gestures of an orator, was now the province of performers who could no longer be called merely 'players'. What these men were now doing was distinctive enough to require that new term to describe it. 'A relatively new art of characterisation had developed', an art to be distinguished from an oratorical display of passion, or an academic actor's portrayal of character types. Gurr quotes Heywood's *Apology for Actors* (1612): the good actor should 'qualify everything according to the nature of the person personated'.

It is obvious that the acting style suited to Marlowe's *Tamburlaine* (1590) or to the *Henry VI* plays and much of *Titus Andronicus* must have been more demonstrative, more emphatic, than the manner appropriate to the soliloquies of Hamlet or of Angelo in *Measure for Measure* (1604) or of *Macbeth* (1606). For example, one will look in vain in the early plays for verse resembling that of this conversation between Achilles and Ulysses in *Troilus and Cressida*. Like Hamlet before his teasing conversation with Polonius (II.ii.167ff.), Ulysses has a book in his hand, and ensures that Achilles should accost him and ask what he is reading:

> ULYSSES   A strange fellow here
> Writes me that man, how dearly ever parted,

How much in having, or without or in,
Cannot make boast to have that which he hath,
Nor feels not what he owes, but by reflection;
As when his virtues, aiming upon others,
Heat them, and they retort that heat again
To the first giver.

ACHILLES   This is not strange, Ulysses.
The beauty that is borne here in the face
The bearer knows not, but commends itself
To others' eyes; nor doth the eye itself,
That most pure spirit of sense, behold itself,
Not going from itself; but eye to eye opposed,
Salutes each other with each other's form;
For speculation turns not to itself,
Till it hath travell'd and is mirror'd there
Where it may see itself. This is not strange at all.

(III.iii.95ff.)

Admittedly, this passage is from a play that depends more than any other on this kind of dialogue; Ulysses is a trickster, but here he tempts Achilles into thoughtful and apparently disinterested argument. Indeed, this play is in a way the most philosophical of them all, even though there are always ironic undertones in the debating; it meditates on the nature of value, but also on meditations about value. There is plenty of personation – that Ulysses should be trying to put something over on Achilles is what one expects, but it is less foreseeable that he should trick the soldier, not primarily associated with thoughtfulness, into such a discussion. Yet Achilles replies in kind, and that gives a new dimension to the character.

To make the point more obvious still, here is a representative passage from the first history sequence, in which Clifford is advising King Henry to show no mercy to his enemies:

> To whom do lions cast their gentle looks?
> Not to the beast that would usurp their den.
> Whose hand is that the forest bear would lick?
> Not his that spoils her young before her face.
> Who scapes the lurking serpent's mortal sting?
> Not he that sets his foot upon her back.
> The smallest worm will turn, being trodden on,
> And doves will peck in safeguard of their brood.
>
> (3 *Henry VI* II.ii.11–18)

This goes on for quite a while. The early history plays contain many orations of this kind, a single point being enforced with multiple illustrations. The difference from the speech of, say, Lady Macbeth is enormous, and it is easy to guess that there must have been an accompanying alteration in acting styles. Not only the actors but the audience had to come to terms with this great change. It was an audience we might describe as oral, as compared with later audiences more accustomed to script; their first training was presumably on sermons and other formalized public speech. So habituated, they could be happy with this leisurely description of a character ringed by his enemies and doomed:

> Environed he was with many foes,
> And stood against them, as the hope of Troy
> Against the Greeks that would have enter'd Troy.
> But Hercules himself must yield to odds;
> And many strokes, though with a little axe,
> Hews down and fells the hardest-timber'd oak.
>
> (II.i.50–5)

There is a passage in *King John* (a play of uncertain date and mixed styles) that sounds almost like a parody of this early manner. Salisbury is vainly trying to persuade the King not to insist on a second coronation:

> Therefore, to be possess'd with double pomp,
> To guard a title that was rich before,
> To gild refined gold, to paint the lily,
> To throw a perfume on the violet,
> To smooth the ice, or add another hue
> Unto the rainbow, or with taper-light
> To seek the beauteous eye of heaven to garnish,
> Is wasteful and ridiculous excess.
>
> (IV.ii.9–16)

This is almost a case of self-irony, for Salisbury's criticism of the King applies to the speech in which he makes it. *King John* is a strange play and contains passages which are more in the later manner, but if it belongs, as it may, to 1594 or thereabouts, this passage is a kind of farewell to a way of speaking that had once seemed perfectly appropriate but now sounds like 'wasteful and ridiculous excess'.

It is worth noting that this mode of writing resembles the way in which non-dramatic narrative was written, albeit at a higher level of achievement. Shakespeare's *The Rape of Lucrece*, written in 1593–4 and so probably almost contemporary with *King John*, can provide the evidence. There is the important difference that the poem is in rhymed stanzas, but the manner of illustrating a point is similar. Lucrece, after the rape, speaks an elaborate condemnation of Night, Time and Opportunity (meaning the chance that made the rape possible):

> O Opportunity, thy guilt is great!
> 'Tis thou that execut'st the traitor's treason;
> Thou sets the wolf where he the lamb may get;
> Whoever plots the sin, thou point'st the season;
> 'Tis thou that spurn'st at right, at law, at reason,
>> And in thy shady cell, where none may spy him,
>> Sits Sin, to seize the souls that wander by him.
>
> (876–82)

This address to Opportunity continues for forty-two more lines, all ingenious, all 'artificial' in the complimentary Elizabethan sense of the word, and then Lucrece turns her attention to Time, with ninety-eight more lines, and very fine they are. Lucrece illustrates her complaint with a long allusion to the fall of Troy as depicted in a tapestry – it was fashionable to include a description of an artwork in the long poems, or epyllia, of the time. *Lucrece* probably suited the taste of Southampton, to whom it was dedicated, yet its procedures are not unlike those of the drama of the period. All that would change when the theatres re-established themselves after the plague years; the audience, always good listeners, were induced or educated to attend to less expansive, knottier verse.

> If it were done, when 'tis done, then 'twere well
> It were done quickly. If th' assassination
> Could trammel up the consequence, and catch
> With his surcease, success; that but this blow
> Might be the be-all and the end-all – here,
> But here, upon this bank and shoal of time,
> We'ld jump the life to come. But in these cases
> We still have judgement here, that we but teach
> Bloody instructions, which, being taught, return

To plague th' inventor. This even-handed justice
Commends th' ingredience of our poison'd chalice
To our own lips…

(Macbeth I.vii.1–12)

What has happened between 1594 and 1606, the date of *Macbeth*? It is hardly too much to call it a revolutionary change in dramatic language, even a transformation of English itself, now alive to a whole new range of poetic possibilities. But 1606 is still some years ahead of us, so we return to 1594.

Among the plays Shakespeare is thought to have added to the
repertoire of the new company were *Titus Andronicus* and *The
Comedy of Errors*, his first tragedy and his first comedy – each
in its way a learned work – and since he brought history plays
as well, he had already tried his hand at the three genres that
would occupy him henceforth. *Titus* is a horror play, now generally accepted to have been written in collaboration with
George Peele. It is full of wickedness, of rapes, murders and
amputations, with a mad revenger and a great deal of rhetorical
display. In one extraordinary scene Lavinia, raped, her tongue
cut out and her hands lopped off, meets her uncle Marcus, who
greets her with a speech describing her condition in forty-seven
ornate lines, of which the purpose is to get her to explain how
she got into such a state; then follows a belated recognition
that she is in no position to do so. In the course of his oration
Marcus remembers the similar plight of Philomela, raped by
Tereus in the story by Ovid which is at the root of the play:

> A craftier Tereus, cousin, thou hast met,
> And he has cut those pretty fingers off
> That could have better sew'd than Philomel.
> O had the monster seen those lily hands
> Tremble like aspen leaves upon a lute,
> And made the silken strings delight to kiss them,

He would not then have touch'd them for his life!

(II.iv.41–7)

And so on.

Since the twentieth-century revival of interest in this play, stimulated by Peter Brook's famous production of 1955, directors have found several different ways of doing this scene without inviting ridicule; and scholars have found ways of justifying it. But John Kerrigan offers an especially interesting argument that there is a natural affinity between revenge tragedy and the ridiculous. *Titus* is packed with farcical moments, culminating in the Thyestean banquet at which Titus plays the cook and has these climactic lines in response to an inquiry as to where Tamora's wicked sons, the rapists, may be: 'Why, there they are, both baked in that pie / Whereof their mother daintily hath fed' (V.iii.60–1). Here and elsewhere horror turns to laughter. As Kerrigan remarks, 'Sour wit and giggling sadism are recurrent traits of the revenger', and so is the kind of craziness that animates the desperate Titus. Part of the interest lies in the choices an audience must make from time to time between pity and incredulous laughter. That must have been, in *Titus* as in other plays, including such majestic instances of the genre as *Hamlet*, part of the appeal of this long-lasting though ever-changing fashion. And it is important to note that the first audience in all probability would not have included Marcus's speech among the items that made them giggle. Shakespeare is making poetry of a recognizable kind about the extraordinary appearance of Lavinia, and he is making it just as he would have done if this were not a play but a non-dramatic poem like *Lucrece*. Such a poem can make no provision for silence, which can be a powerful element in drama. So Marcus must talk and talk, like some characters in the history plays; by the time of *Richard III* the rhetoric is more varied, the approach to personation closer. Shakespeare never again wrote as he did in *Titus Andronicus*, though he wrote bombast when it was called for, not only for fun, as in the language of Pistol, but for serious purposes, as in the characterization of Othello.

The Comedy of Errors is also a learned play, but in a different way. It is known to have been performed at Gray's Inn, one of the Inns of Court, during the Christmas celebrations of 1594, though it had probably been in existence two or three years before that. The *Gesta Grayorum*, which reported such revels for the benefit of posterity, remarked that so many people attended the play that 'there was no convenient room for the actors'. There was much disorder, but when the crowd thinned, 'a Comedy of Errors (like to Plautus his *Menaechmus*)' was enacted. The scholars of the Inn, in their carnival mode, would at once have spotted the relationship of this play to that of Plautus. No translation existed, but many, including the author, would have read the play in Latin, for the second-century dramatist and his coeval Terence were much taught in Elizabethan schools; indeed, Terence and his commentators were also the accepted authority on dramatic structure. This short work of Plautus was often adapted for the modern stage. Shakespeare was free to re-handle the plot and add scenes with no counterpart in the original, as when the husband is locked out while the wife dines with his double.

The errors (almost a technical term) are the false or deceptive recognitions which propel the plot. In the best Renaissance manner, Shakespeare sought to outdo or 'over-go' his model by having not one but two pairs of twins. He also sets the comic action within a romance plot that he would return to in his last years, especially in *Pericles*. The result is a mixture of romance and smart Roman comedy that owes as much to the English as to the classical tradition.

G. K. Hunter looks back from this comedy to an earlier one, the *Supposes* of George Gascoigne, performed at Gray's Inn in 1566. It is a translation of a play by Ariosto, and the plot turns on the familiar errors or deceptions; but Hunter remarks that the gap between Gascoigne's play and Shakespeare's 'measures the whole story of Elizabethan commercial drama. By the time of Shakespeare's play there was a well-founded professional theatre in London with a considerable repertory and a sophisticated technique to express the nuance of individual experience.' Developments of this and other kinds continued, as I have suggested; we reach the apogee of Elizabethan drama later, when Shakespeare's plays were done at the Globe. Softening the hard Roman story with the romance tale of Aegeon, *The Comedy of Errors* shows that English comedy was equipped for a brilliant future, using the past but free in its own powers of invention, popular with the learned students of the Inns but remaining in touch with native traditions of entertainment.

But where there was change, there was also continuity. The anonymous play *Mucedorus* (1588), with its banal romance plot, remained popular and was revived by Shakespeare's company, in a slightly revised form, when he was working on the late plays that are also known as romances, though belonging to a far higher state of refinement. It seems that *Mucedorus* could please an audience that could also accept *The Winter's Tale*. And it was essential to please that popular audience, at least until the company began to exploit the Blackfriars. The

Inns of Court must also be catered to, but if the Globe ever had a full house and an attendance of three thousand, it is a safe bet that around 2700 of them were not scholars, not the kind of auditors Gabriel Harvey had in mind when he remarked that *Hamlet* was a play to 'please the wiser sort'. It had to please others not warranting that description. Consequently the respect for classical antecedents – Ovid, Seneca, Plautus – had to be consistent with the telling of a good story; and the dramatists, valuing their freedom as well as their obligation, ignored these august precedents whenever they felt it advisable to do so. So a play that is based on a tragic story, and begins tragically, may have a happy ending (*The Winter's Tale*, for instance), and English writers wrote tragicomedy without consulting elaborate Italian theories about that genre. What kind of play is *Cymbeline*? The Folio of 1623, where it makes its first appearance in print, includes it among the tragedies. Nowadays it is usually called a romance. It is partly a history play, dealing with ancient Britain and the Roman occupation. It is not a proper tragicomedy because the rules maintained that in tragicomedy characters may be brought close to death but must not die. But Cloten dies; and in another romance, *The Winter's Tale*, Mamillius dies. *Troilus and Cressida* is described by the publishers both as a tragedy and as a comedy. *Measure for Measure* is set on an apparently unstoppably tragic course and ends with everybody getting married. People did not care greatly for narrow prescriptions of decorum. What mattered was the power of language to delight, whatever the dramatic circumstances.

It appears that between 1594 and 1598, when the Globe opened, Shakespeare was engaged mostly on comedies and on a new cycle of history plays. The chronology is uncertain, but

The Taming of the Shrew and *The Two Gentlemen of Verona* either existed already or were written about 1594, with *Love's Labour's Lost* played in the following year, and perhaps with revisions in 1597; this was the only play in the group to be published in the poet's lifetime (1598). The second history tetralogy began with *Richard II* in 1595, and *1 Henry IV* and *2 Henry IV* followed within the next couple of years. The last play of the four, *Henry V*, can be dated to 1599 with exceptional confidence by its flattering reference to Essex in Ireland, and its reference to the 'wooden O', which is likely to refer to the Globe, the proud new theatre opened the year before.

Bundling all these plays together may give some notion of the fecundity of Shakespeare in his early thirties, yet there is also *King John*, probably a reworking of an older play, as well as part of the banned play *Sir Thomas More* (1593), mainly by Anthony Munday; the manuscript survives and contains a section of three pages confidently asserted to be in Shakespeare's hand. It seems that he was, even in such a busy time, willing to help in a work of multiple composition. *Romeo and Juliet* and its comic twin *A Midsummer Night's Dream* are dated 1595, and somehow the extra Falstaff piece *The Merry Wives of Windsor* was produced in 1597 or thereabouts, traditionally said to have been produced on the order of the Queen. At least some of the Sonnets also belong to this ferociously busy period.

Shakespeare was then living a presumably bachelor life in Bishopsgate, not too far from the Theatre. Of his private life very little is known, though the Sonnets fuel a great variety of conjectures. We can harmlessly suppose that in these years, when so much of his time was devoted to the fortunes of the English monarchy, Shakespeare was as aware as any other intelligent person of the uneasy state of the kingdom – the Queen old and difficult, the succession still in question, Essex increasingly dangerous. Then there was the daily evidence of unstoppable inflation, and the intermittent ravages of the plague, which was disastrous for business as well as privately alarming. Perhaps his reaction was to work even harder.

Among the comedies of this period, *The Shrew* may be the one least pleasing to the modern eye and ear. It needs to be read or watched without reference to modern feminism, and one should also remember that the taming of Katherina takes place in a play within a play, which puts the story at another remove from reality. Shrews like Katherina are part of folklore, and the play recognizes that, but develops the story as an elaborate game in which Katherina is tamed exactly like a hawk. She is 'watched', or kept awake, and given food from which the substance has been washed out. The great test for the trainer comes when he lets the bird fly without the 'creance' or cord that has attached it to him during the earlier phases of training. Will it return to his glove when called? Kate does so. The best insight into these tricks is T. H. White's book *The Goshawk*, in which he tells how he tried to tame a German goshawk by methods prescribed in an Elizabethan treatise on hawking. It was an extremely arduous job – for one thing, you have to keep awake in order to keep the bird awake – and White's first attempt failed when the hawk proved 'haggard' and flew downwind, never to be recovered. (One recalls Othello's threat 'If I do prove her haggard, / Though that her jesses were my dear heart-strings / I'd whistle her off, and let her down the wind / To prey at fortune' [III.iii.260–3]. Jesses were the straps that fastened the hawk to the falconer's leash.) What is tragic in the tragedy is comic in the comedy. Katherina behaves like an untrained hawk, 'bating' (a mad rush of angry activity, endangering the precious integrity of the feathers) and generally resisting the trainer, until at last tamed into the condition of a model wife, returning to the glove of the trainer without the aid of the creance. One needs to see the wife-taming in the light of this elaborate joke, which would have been appreciated by the groundlings as easily as a modern audience would accept a comic football metaphor.

The Two Gentlemen of Verona is a slight work, but it has many pretty verses. It is Italian in style and theme, a conflict between the love of male friends and the love of women; the friends become amorous rivals, one crooked and one straight. They have each a servant, one smart, the other comically dull. It has the look of a play meant for a more gentle audience than the Theatre would normally attract, except that the humour of Launce and his dog Crab does speak to popular taste. The play is a source of wonder only if one considers the easy lyric sweetness of much of the verse; it sounds like the work of one who specialized in that style. But it came from the same hand that had recently written *Richard III* and that would, in little more than a decade, be writing the bleak and complicated verse of *Coriolanus*.

Of the early comedies the finest, strangest, and in many ways the most difficult to the modern audience is *Love's Labour's Lost*. It makes allusion, not always very plainly, to recent political issues, and in particular reflects a contemporary aristocratic French fashion: the lords withdraw from the world into their private academy. Some of the characters bear the names of real people: Navarre became King Henri IV; Biron, a celebrated French general, was an associate of the Earl of Essex; Longaville had been governor of Normandy as recently as 1591. The unwelcome visit of the royal ladies recalls that of Catherine de Medici with her daughter and a company of witty women. The title page of the Quarto published in 1598 rightly calls it 'a pleasant conceited comedy'.

An obviously courtly play, *Love's Labour's Lost* was acted before the Queen in the Christmas celebrations of the previous year, and at Southampton's house when he was released from prison in 1604; but it was also done at the Globe. It may not have been fully understood by that seemingly voracious public, and it is certainly not understood in every detail today. It is an old guess that Holofernes was a satirical portrait of the pedantic Gabriel Harvey and Mote a caricature of Harvey's real-life opponent, clever, witty Thomas Nashe, whose novel *The Unfortunate Traveller* (1594) was dedicated to Southampton. There are in the play obscurities that suggest it had meanings fully accessible only to a few. A favourite theory is that Biron (Berowne) is attacking a group of savants known as the School of Night, or by some the School of Atheism, who were very interested in mathematics, the new astronomy, and various kinds of occultism. The School is said to have included Raleigh and 'the wizard earl' of Northumberland, as well as the poet Chapman, translator of Homer, believed by some to have been the Rival Poet of the Sonnets and the author of the splendidly obscure poems *The Shadow of Night* and *Ovid's Banquet of Sense*. But the chief brain of the group is said to have been Thomas Hariot, a dependant of Raleigh's and a man of versatile genius – navigator, astronomer, maker of horoscopes, and an early smoker. The existence of a School of Night, so called, depends heavily on a line of Berowne's about 'the hue of dungeons and the school of night' (IV.iii.251), in which the reading and sense of 'school' are debatable. Nevertheless such groups of students did exist. They had a reputation for far-out learning but also for pedantry and dullness, and they were therefore disliked by more sprightly men who were more interested in wit and poetry.

The appeal of the play being in some degree topical, it must inevitably contain references to coteries and in-jokes now beyond recovery. One guess at its origin, a guess as good as any other, is Anthony Holden's theory that the French court setting stands for Southampton's 'cultured, if playful, household, where the study (and production) of literature was constantly interrupted by amorous intrigues'. Berowne may stand for the young and frisky Shakespeare himself, and there is a notably sexy Dark Lady. Dr Johnson, who may have picked up more double entendres than we can, said that the play was full of passages that were mean, childish and vulgar, passages that should not have been spoken before a 'maiden queen'.

Still, if we allow for the fact that much is going on that we can't quite follow, the play remains a brilliant achievement, and it is worth remembering that it seems to have pleased everybody from the Queen to the Globe audience. It represents a world of delightful artifice, a world in which, as in the early passages of *Romeo and Juliet* a little later on, characters speak easily in sonnet form, or produce great bursts of courtly eloquence, inflated but deflatable. It uses much more rhyme than any other of the plays, but also controls dialects less glorious than those of the gentlemen – the boastful soldier, the witty servant, the first in a line of malaprop constables. Beneath the bravura display a serious language game is being played, evidence that the story is not wholly of charming and artificial manners. Berowne's protest to the King against the very idea of prolonged celibate study – 'every man with his affects is born, /

Not with might master'd but with special grace' (I.i.151–2) – makes a genuine theological point: feats of this kind, achieving mastery over the passions, cannot be achieved by man's unaided effort but only by the prior intervention of the grace of God. They are not to be had merely by exerting the will against 'the huge army of the world's desires' (I.i.10). One notices the repeated apposition of the words 'wit' and 'will'. Maria says of Longaville that he has 'a sharp wit match'd with too blunt a will' (II.i.49) and adds 'Whose edge hath power to cut, whose will still wills / It should none spare'. The word 'will' is forced on our attention by the paradox, that although it is blunt it cuts. 'Wit' has the fuller Elizabethan sense, implying the full power of the mind. Philip Sidney in his *Apology for Poetry* speaks of 'erected wit, infected will' – a terse bit of theology embodying the idea that the actions of the proud intellect are corrupted by sin; we return to Berowne's point that man is fallen and can be saved only by special grace. The word 'will' is used in a specialized sense in the Sonnets and elsewhere to mean 'sexual desire', or even to refer to the sexual organs. The antithesis 'wit/will' is also used by Katharine when she says that Dumaine has 'wit to make an ill shape good, / And shape to win grace though he had no wit' (II.i.59–60).

There are better ways of deserving grace than by academic labour, or the affectation of it. Just as 'wit' covers both verbal ingenuity and the general power of the mind, so 'grace' can refer to physical beauty without parting from its theological sense. From 1571 the *Book of Common Prayer*, so formative of English Protestantism, included, as number X of the Thirty-nine Articles of Religion, this advice: 'We have no power to do good works pleasant and acceptable to God, without the grace of God by Christ preventing us, that we may have good will' to repent, to be born again. 'Preventing' is used in the old sense of 'going before' – giving the grace necessary to man, who, being fallen, could only sin. This grace was called, using an expression of St Augustine's, 'prevenient grace', which is in God's gift and not dependent on the merit of the recipient. This supports Berowne's original plea: victory against the huge army of the world's desires cannot be had by an unaided act of will. The point is made more simply by the botanizing Friar in *Romeo and Juliet:* 'Two such opposed kings encamp them still / In man as well as herbs – grace and rude will' (II.iii.27–8). Underneath the banter and wit of the play there is solid theological ground. In an age so habituated to religious controversy the point would have been much more easily taken than in our less theological age. 'Affect' is blind; even when the lords have declared in favour of love and the world they do so to the wrong women: 'We are again forsworn, in will and error' (V.ii.471). And when the scene darkens with the arrival of Marcade, bearer of the bad news of mortality, the young men are dismissed to penance and the corporal works of mercy, being required to

> Visit the speechless sick, and still converse
> With groaning wretches; and your task shall be,
> With all the fierce endeavour of your wit,
> To enforce the pained impotent to smile.

> (V.ii.851–4)

Visiting the sick and tending prisoners were two of the seven Corporal Works of Mercy. If the theology has the flavour of Reform, the tasks here imposed remember the customs of the old faith.

The virtues of this play give abundant promise of future

versatility and depth. It was followed by *A Midsummer Night's Dream*, which can be considered along with its tragic antithesis *Romeo and Juliet*, both written about 1595–6. There is general agreement that the *Dream* was written for, or at any rate performed at, some grand wedding, and various such occasions have been proposed, but none has prevailed; while private performance is of course perfectly possible, we should still think of the play as having, like all or almost all of the others, a life in the public theatre, well away from grand aristocratic occasions.

As in *Love's Labour's Lost* one notes – and this becomes too obvious to bear repetition – the variety of dialects used; the young lovers do not talk like Theseus and Hippolyta, the artisans and the fairies have their own languages. A small price has to be paid for this multiplicity – the verse of the young lovers is often rather insipid; but these persons, hormone-dominated and too immature for grown-up passion, must be seen to have a certain triviality. Like *Romeo and Juliet* (in which diversity of dialect is more firmly controlled), the *Dream* is partly based on the story of Pyramus and Thisbe. We are warned at the outset, in the dialogue between Hermia and Lysander, that 'quick bright things come to confusion' (I.i.149), but in the comedy they of course do not, except in Bottom's play, which virtually repeats, in the mode of farce, the tragedy of *Romeo and Juliet*.

The *Dream* is a festive comedy, appropriately set on Midsummer Eve, the vigil of St John the Baptist, when it was the custom, deplored by Puritan writers and preachers, for young persons of both sexes to withdraw to the woods for their pleasure. The word 'dote', a pejorative synonym for 'love', occurs frequently in connection with the young couples; Puck, lacking human 'affect', identifies their behaviour as madness, and their loves are febrile and shallow compared with the grown-up affections of Theseus and Hippolyta. To allow one's conduct to be decided on the evidence of the eye uncontrolled by the judgement is to risk disaster; eyes are often mentioned in this play because (according to the song in *The Merchant of Venice*) it is in the eye that love is engendered (III.ii.67). From the eye it descends to the organs of the lower senses, unless the eye is made the basis of a Platonic ascent – a development of no interest to these lovers.

The combinations of the plot are comparable with those of the language. There is even a sense in which the sub-plot of Bottom and his friends is the main plot, and the performance of the Pyramus play, with the final appearance of Puck and the fairies, actually brings everything together. It turns out that of all the characters Bottom had the clearest understanding of the metamorphoses of love, vouchsafed him in a dream, as happened to the hero in Apuleius's ancient novel *The Golden Ass*. His bewildered acknowledgement of the favour of the goddess is rendered as a rather daring parody of St Paul's words in 1 Corinthians 2:9 – 'Eye hath not seen, nor ear heard, neither have entered into the heart of man the things which God hath prepared for them that love him.' So St Paul; and now Bottom: 'The eye of man hath not heard, the ear of man hath not seen, man's hand is not able to taste, his tongue to conceive, nor his heart to report, what my dream was' (IV.i.204–14). Paul is clear that this is wisdom, though it is a wisdom denied and thought folly by 'the princes of this world'. The auditor needed to pick up the fantasticated allusion to St Paul; but by this time we can reasonably suppose that the audience contained many Bible readers. They would enjoy the idea of Bottom having seen something of 'the deep things of God' which were denied his betters, the princes who would ridicule his play.

The *Dream* is certainly among the intellectual and dramaturgical triumphs of the playwright's early career. *Romeo* matches it in that it has continued to please and offers as it were an alternative ending to and a new valuation of young love. It has often been criticized for lacking the inevitability supposed to be necessary to tragedy – the disaster happens because of a series of accidents. Yet the play opens with a sonnet, spoken by the Chorus, that clearly presages doom for the star-crossed lovers, speaking of 'the children's end' as the product of their 'parents' strife'. The antithetical relation of love to strife persists throughout, and so does the part of luck, or the stars. The orderliness of the recurring sonnet form extends the pathos; here are moments of grace and order in the midst of brawling and duelling. So, as the sister play predicted, quick bright things may come to confusion.

At the outset Romeo is in a melancholy amorous daze about a girl, whom, fittingly, we never see. It is a youthful pose or attitude. The vivacity and aggressiveness of Mercutio and Tybalt demonstrate youthful energy used otherwise, and now the posing is of male challenge and insult, displayed as mindless in the opening lines of dialogue between servants of the rival houses. So, too, the Petrarchan extravagances of the hero are set against a background of sexual coarseness, Mercutio's and the Nurse's. There are bawdiness and brawling, solemnity and wantonness, antitheses of youth and age, peace and fighting, love and lust. Old Capulet sits with Paris planning a sober bourgeois wedding while Romeo and Juliet make love in the same house; Juliet rapturously invokes the coming night as Tybalt, whose death prevents that happiness, lies dead in the street.

Shakespeare turns away from his source, the long and

tedious *Tragical History of Romeus and Juliet* by Arthur
Brooke (1562), and declines to make the story a warning to
lovers against 'thralling themselves to unhonest desire,
neglecting authority and advice of friends', though Elizabethan
parents of the same social standing as the Capulets would certainly, in their own lives, instruct their daughters to accept the
likes of Paris and expect to be obeyed. And indeed Shakespeare
provides a love so likely to earn the shocked disapproval of the
old people with a fatal consequence; but in its way that love
has become suddenly and even admirably mature. Romeo
abandons the artificial language that goes with his youthful
posing, and as his language clears, Juliet also becomes a plain
speaker: 'Fain would I dwell on form, fain, fain, deny / What I
have spoke, but farewell compliment' (II.ii.88–9). When they
first meet at the Capulet party they converse in a sonnet, but
they soon move to monosyllabic plainness: 'I would not for the
world they saw thee here' (II.ii.74). When Romeo is forced to
believe that Juliet is dead he avoids the lengthy lamentation
that would have been appropriate in *Titus Andronicus*; he
moves briskly into action, ordering horses, remembering an
apothecary, expressing his grief almost calmly: 'Well, Juliet, I
will lie with thee tonight' (V.i.34). For contrast we have the
absurd laments of the Nurse and the Capulets over Juliet's
body, supposed dead (IV.v).

We have considered above some of the political aspects of
Richard II, a play close in date to *Romeo and Juliet*. It was published as a Quarto in 1597. Not all plays reached publication,
even when the companies had given up performing them, and
of those that did appear as books, not many went into the editions beyond the first that made the stationer-publisher his

75

profit. But this play had five editions in the author's lifetime and another in 1634. The deposition scene, at first omitted, appeared in the fourth edition of 1608, and thereafter. The play was evidently popular as a reading text. But, as we gathered from the testimony of the actor at the inquiry into the production commissioned for Essex, it was out of theatrical use by 1601. The subject – the usurpation of a weak and self-indulgent monarch, who happened to be the last to have an undisputed claim to the throne – was a dangerous one to enact, even allowing for the fact that the censor was on the whole generous in his response to history plays that might perhaps have been expected to upset him. As always, Shakespeare drew on various chronicle histories, but he must also have had in mind Marlowe's *Edward II* (1591–2), another account of the fate of a weak king in the power of favourites. Marlowe's play was also popular, and an edition had appeared in 1594.

It is not difficult to understand the interest shown in these kings, both thought homosexual and both indulgent to favourites. In some respects their weaknesses foreshadowed some of those attributed to the present aged incumbent. Moreover the plays dealt with questions of deposition and succession, topics disagreeable to the Queen, who was not short of enemies who wanted to depose and succeed her. Shakespeare had already written the series of four plays in which the narrative culminated in the crowning of Henry Tudor, Elizabeth's grandfather. Now he embarked on another series that would end with the triumph of Henry V, who inherited the throne from the usurper Bolingbroke, and was the father of the unhappy Henry VI.

Richard II is complete in itself, and the king is virtually the first of the tragic heroes of whom we discover an inner as well as a public life. His bad record as a ruler is duly recorded, and Bolingbroke scarcely needs Machiavellian skills to get rid of him. Yet Richard seduces the audience with the tune of his voice. Sometimes affected and self-pitying, it nevertheless imposes itself on the auditor's mind:

> What must the King do now? Must he submit?
> The King shall do it. Must he be depos'd?
> The King shall be contented. Must he lose
> The name of king? A' God's name let it go.
> I'll give my jewels for a set of beads,
> My gorgeous palace for a hermitage,
> My gay apparel for an almsman's gown,
> My figur'd goblets for a dish of wood,
> My sceptre for a palmer's walking-staff,
> My subjects for a pair of carved saints;
> And my large kingdom for a little grave,
> A little little grave, an obscure grave –
> Or I'll be buried in the king's high way,
> Some way of common trade, where subjects' feet
> May hourly trample on their sovereign's head;
> For on my heart they tread now whilst I live,
> And buried once, why not upon my head?
>
> (III.iii.143–59)

This pathos serves a double purpose: it touches the hearers but at the same time convinces them that self-pity is not a quality to be admired in a monarch. It is founded in a sense of violated privilege, with no thought whatever of obligation. Richard makes much of this kind of rhetoric. Yet when we see him at the end of the play the effect is changed. Here the King speaks the first of Shakespeare's great soliloquies. He had used

soliloquy before, but never with this effect of serious meditation. It tells of a man trying to understand his place in a world
that is no longer his to play with. Still impregnated with self-
pity, the speech is nevertheless the first that at least hints at
the range and power of Hamlet's soliloquies, or Macbeth's or
Angelo's. It is too long to quote in full; here are a few lines of
it:

> I have been studying how I may compare
> This prison where I live unto the world,
> And for because the world is populous,
> And here is not a creature but myself,
> I cannot do it; yet I'll hammer it out.
> My brain I'll prove the female to my soul,
> My soul the father, and these two beget
> A generation of still-breeding thoughts;
> And these same thoughts people this little world:
> For no thought is contented. The better sort,
> As thoughts of things divine, are intermix'd
> With scruples, and do set the word itself
> Against the word.
> As thus: 'Come, little ones,' and then again
> 'It is as hard to come as for a camel
> To thread the postern of a small needle's eye.' ...
>   Whate'er I be,
> Nor I nor any man that but man is,
> With nothing shall be pleas'd, till he be eas'd
> With being nothing.
>
>   (V.v.1–41)

Note the complexity, with its suggestion of self-regard, in the
rhymes and antitheses of the last four lines. It may be that the

need to represent – to provide for the personation of – a king so full of tender self-regard made the inwardness of those later soliloquies possible. It opened up a new rhetorical range, a range that Shakespeare was to explore almost alone. The grammatical concision of the lines looks forward to greater things in the future.

The remaining plays of the tetralogy – the two parts of *Henry IV* and the last play, *Henry V* – were probably written just before and just after the move to the Globe, between 1597 and 1599. *Henry V* seems to celebrate the new theatre, even when dwelling on its inadequacy to the task of representing a great patriotic war. All the plays are, inevitably, political. The relation between the first two has been much disputed, and it does appear that the second is not a straightforward historical sequel; it begins where the first part ends, but the relationship between the king and his son has been moved back, as if Hal's demonstration of nobility and valour at the battle of Shrewsbury had not yet been made. There remain rebels to be destroyed, and Falstaff, less attractive and amusing in the second part, has to be formally dismissed from the circle of the new king. His shaming encounter with the Lord Chief Justice, and his cold rejection by King Henry, are necessary, since the wanton prince must become the just, virtuous, and serious monarch; but it strikes many as a merciless bit of playwriting. And there remains a sense that political history, with its undertones of guilt in this royal house, and the scenes depicting Hal's riotous youth, at times sit uneasily together.

The rhetorical riches of the play lie in the characters of Hotspur and Falstaff. Hotspur is mad about honour, and sounds it; he rants and swaggers like Essex, but when confronted by the ineffective magical posturings of Glendower he becomes a defender of the plain style, and he is given a chance to explain his preference when he tells the Welsh leader that he 'had rather hear a brazen canstick turn'd, / Or a dry wheel grate on the axle-tree, / And that would set my teeth nothing an edge, / Nothing so much as mincing poetry' (III.i.129–32). The theme is repeated in his attack on the fop he meets on the battlefield (I.iii.36–56).

Of Falstaff it is unnecessary to say very much, since he is legendary: a witty fraud, his selfishness and riot are so evident that he has to be taken as a cause of amusement rather than a target for censure. It is all so well done that one actually feels sorry for him when he loses his false friend the Prince and for-feits the thousand pounds – an enormous sum – that he owes to Shallow, another extraordinary comic creation. All Falstaff's fun and games coexist with a moral outcome so disagreeably managed that an audience may well find itself on the side of riotous behaviour. The coexistence of moral and immoral material is part of the texture of these plays, though contrary to contemporary official opinion on morality in literature.

So, too, in *Henry V*, which has to combine a patriotic cele-bration of its hero with a continuing interest (referred to by the King himself) in the consequences of the crime by which Richard II was ousted. The play also has a serious debate between the King and the soldier Williams on a matter of ethical importance; Williams will not exempt him from the crime of slaughtering his men in an unjust cause. The play allows us to see that it is at odds with itself – the dialogue with Williams hardly illustrates the virtues proclaimed by the Chorus at the beginning of Act IV:

O now, who will behold
The royal captain of this ruin'd band
Walking from watch to watch, from tent to tent,
Let him cry 'Praise and glory on his head!'

(IV *Chorus* 28–31)

That 'little touch of Harry in the night' (47) which, it is claimed, will ease the troops in their hunger and fatigue did not have the desired effect on the thoughtful foot-soldier Williams. Here is one of the moments when Shakespeare can make us feel out of our depth: the part of the surly Williams is so strongly written, his arguments so persuasive compared with Henry's, that we are left querying our assent to the royal cause, however warmly solicited.

Despite the promises given in the Epilogue to *2 Henry IV*, there was no place for Falstaff in *Henry V*, only the reports of his illness and then of his death, in a few famous lines of comic mourning spoken by Mistress Quickly. Falstaff's demise might have been got over more easily, but it became an occasion for pathos and drollery; when she offers her intimate, funny account of the old man's death (II.iii.9–20) we have not yet forgotten her earlier, simpler words: 'The King has kill'd his heart' (II.i.88). It is amusing to think of the company conference at which it was decided to leave Falstaff out of this play, with subsequent discussion as to how an audience aware of the previous promise might be satisfied. The way to write Falstaff out of the series was to let him die; but even that expedient called for some scrap of story, and it needed comic delicacy in the handling. It was understandably left to Shakespeare to see to this.

Despite recent attempts to give it immediate political

importance as providing covert support for Essex in a move to support the succession of James VI of Scotland, *Henry V* is not now among the plays thought most interesting, though it had its moment in the Second World War, and one aspect of it, now less animating, is well represented by the patriotic fervour of the Olivier film. Leaving considerations of fashion aside, *Henry V* is certainly worth attention as testimony to the professional resource of the dramatist. He could do the big shots, kings, dauphins, lords, a French princess given to comic slips when talking English; but with as much conviction he could render the conversation of soldiers from all the four nations and give full expression to the grave arguments of an intelligent dissident infantryman.

The last comedies more or less certainly written before 1598 were *The Merchant of Venice, The Merry Wives of Windsor*, and *Much Ado About Nothing*. One is tempted to dismiss *The Merry Wives* as W. H. Auden did in his series of Shakespeare lectures. Here is the whole text of his lecture: '*The Merry Wives of Windsor* is a very dull play indeed. We can be grateful for its having been written, because it provided the occasion of Verdi's *Falstaff*, a very great operatic masterpiece. Mr Page, Shallow, Slender and the Host disappear. I have nothing to say about Shakespeare's play, so let's hear Verdi.' As Auden had plenty to say about most of the other plays, this amounts to a severe condemnation. He does not ask himself why Boito and Verdi thought it worth the trouble, though their labour was immense and joyous. For all the virtuosity and refinement of the opera, I think Verdi was fascinated above all by Falstaff's fatness, indeed with his grossness generally, as illustrated by the duplicated love letters to the two wives. The English, who have made a folk hero of the fat boy Billy Bunter, find obesity funny, and so, it seems, did Verdi, if his correspondence is a guide; perhaps the joke is even better when the fat person is also lascivious. In any case it seems to me that Auden was right in thinking it took three centuries for this play to find a habitat in which it could flourish.

The reputation of *The Merchant of Venice* is mostly owing to the character of Shylock, who of course is not the merchant but the usurer of Venice; the merchant is Antonio. Shylock has been endlessly and beyond necessity involved in arguments about anti-Semitism. James Shapiro, in his excellent book *Shakespeare and the Jews*, remarks that 'ideas about the Jews that emerged in Shakespeare's lifetime continued to influence notions of Jewish identity' – indeed, the play 'had come to embody English conceptions of Jewish racial and national difference'. Yet there were very few Jews in Shakespeare's London – one estimate is as low as two hundred. They had been officially expelled by Edward I in 1290, and the usual story is that they were readmitted by Cromwell in 1656, though Shapiro thinks this was a relaxation of the rule rather than its abolition. He examines the whole history/myth of Expulsion and Readmission in his Chapter 20. On the whole we may be sure that Shakespeare was thinking first of usury, and then of Jews who traditionally practised it because Christians were forbidden to do so. The religious differences extend and illustrate the difference of opinion about venture and usury.

Shakespeare of course owes a great deal to the folklore that had long attached itself to Jews, much as he does to the old riddle game by which one suitor is preferred to the others; but it may well be true that the contemporary case of the physician Roderigo Lopez was in his mind. Lopez, a Portuguese Jewish physician who attended Queen Elizabeth, was in 1594 tried on false evidence on a charge of plotting the Queen's death by poison, and executed with all the horrors appropriate to the torture and death of traitors – a fate for which he had Essex to thank.

The Jew of myth was a monster, like Marlowe's Barabbas in *The Jew of Malta* (1592). Shylock is not in that class; he is a lonely usurer, something of a miser, the subject of unthinking contempt from Gentiles. His trade was one that Christians, historically uneasy about usury, allowed Jews to practise because somebody must. The central economic theme of the play, that distinction between usury and 'venture', is spelled out in a rather unusual way in the debate about the biblical story of Laban's lambs. Was Jacob cheating when he made sure by a trick that the lambs would be particoloured, and so due to him? Shylock takes the story as a justification for usury, but Antonio regards Jacob as having made a venture: 'This was a venture, sir, that Jacob serv'd for, / A thing not in his power to bring to pass' (I.iii.91–2). Antonio made his money virtuously, without demanding interest, by risking his great ships on foreign voyages; Shylock made money breed, an unnatural thing for metal to be doing. Since the time of Aristotle, usury had been condemned as unnatural, and compared to sodomy. Bassanio's mission to Belmont is a venture, compared to Jason's quest for the Golden Fleece, and Antonio finances it not as a loan at interest but out of love for his friend.

There is an old question as to why a certain melancholy pervades this play from its very first line, Antonio's 'In sooth I know not why I am so sad'. He is sad throughout, even when his ships turn up safe. Portia's first line is 'By my troth, Nerissa, my little body is a-weary of this great world' (I.ii.1).

Even the splendours and riches of Belmont are a little sad. Sometimes it is hard to see in which direction our sympathies are being solicited: for example, are we expected to approve of the conduct of Jessica, a thief and a runaway? While they are in Belmont, Lorenzo speaks a beautiful formal praise of music – *laus musicae* – and that may predispose us towards him; but when he and Jessica perform their duet 'On such a night as this', all the women mentioned are in some way doomed or bad – Cressida, Thisbe, Dido, Medea; and Jessica's name is added to the list (V.i.1–17).

What is extraordinarily effective is the matching of a serious theme with fairy tale, and the effect is always of firm intellectual control. It seems that Shakespeare was now able to take disparate ideas, join them together, and make them penetrate the body of the play, so that there is a sense that gold may be associated with love, pleasure, marriage, and also with a sort of formalized greed, somehow proper to Shylock's business, though he makes it the cause of a bargain that demands flesh in payment for metal, a bargain 'unkind' in all the Elizabethan senses – unnatural as well as ungenerous, and the opposite of Antonio's arrangement with Bassanio. Antonio is well born, that is, gentle (Gentile), but spits ungently on Shylock's gaberdine, an act justified only by Shylock's unavoidable failure to be gentle/Gentile. The differences between them culminate in the trial. The trial is folklore, and the judgement comes from a folklore lawyer, but the issues are real enough, and may justify that air of melancholy. Antonio's opening line is reinforced a little, and in part explained, by Salerio, when he dwells on the risks to Antonio's 'wealthy' ships. If he were Antonio, he asks,

> Should I go to church,
> And see the holy edifice of stone,
> And not bethink me straight of dangerous rocks,
> Which touching but my gentle vessel's side
> Would scatter all her spices on the stream,
> Enrobe the roaring waters with my silks,
> And in a word, but even now worth this,
> And now worth nothing?
>
> (I.i.29–36)

Here, despite the lightness of tone, are the dangers of Antonio's ventures, and the gorgeousness of what would be lost if they were to miscarry. And here is a mercantile figure for the losses that make others besides merchants sad. One notices the intrusive word 'gentle' applied to a ship – a Gentile ship, property of a Christian gentleman, not possibly of a Jewish usurer. It is all myth and allegory; in the Venice of the sixteenth century, Antonio would probably have been buying insurance from very respectable Shylocks, unburdening himself of an anxiety incident to his profession but no longer inevitable.

To conclude this brief survey of the plays written before Shakespeare's company moved into the Globe, a word is needed for *Much Ado About Nothing*, a comedy unlike the others in that it is dependent on a well-maintained flow of witty and varied talk. The main plot – the contrived slander of Hero – is an old one. It will appear to modern audiences that the wicked plotter succeeds in disgracing not the innocent Hero but Claudio, for his condemnation of his bride is coarse and public, and even when he knows her to have been innocent he is apparently unmoved by the report of her death. However, it does not seem that we are invited to think very ill of him. In any case the interest of the play lies, notoriously, in the Beatrice and Benedick story, and this preference may have been felt from the beginning. Charles I took a copy of the Second Folio into captivity – it is now in the library of Windsor Castle – and altered the titles of the plays to suit his preferences, so that *Twelfth Night* is renamed 'Malvolio', and *Much Ado About Nothing* became 'Benedick and Beatrice'. The wit combats of these characters were apparently what always pleased most. More than other comedies of the period, *Much Ado* anticipates the witty duelling of Restoration comedy, perhaps by developing an older Elizabethan style, the courtly comedy of John Lyly, which had been out of fashion for a while.

The incursion of the military had made Messina a holiday place, and the setting is a little like that of *Love's Labour's Lost* except that the women are welcomed rather than accepted as of necessity. The action turns on two tricks, one – John's – wicked, the other, the plots against Benedick and Beatrice, benevolent, and not unlike the plot against Berowne in the earlier comedy. All ends well, but the title looks awry if one considers the ordeal of Hero; unless, as some believe, it is a sexual double entendre, 'nothing' being an Elizabethan slang word for the female genitals.

The play has a high proportion of prose, roughly three-quarters of the whole – not quite as high as in *The Merry Wives*, but about twice as high as in *Love's Labour's Lost*. Presumably prose was best for the easygoing, teasing manner of much of the dialogue. One wonders whether it did not reflect more closely the character of aristocratic conversation in the later years of Elizabeth, as Shakespeare might have heard it in Southampton's circles. Verbal wit, considered an index of intelligence, was highly valued in all the aristocracies of Europe. About the time Shakespeare was writing this comedy, John Donne, called the monarch of wit, was probably at work on his *Songs and Sonnets* and on his no less witty religious poetry. We need not suppose that Elizabeth's courtiers were as witty as Donne, or as Beatrice and Benedick; but they doubtless spoke in lithe and resourceful prose, not altogether remote from what Shakespeare made of it in writing *Much Ado About Nothing.*

The Globe was not the first theatre to be built on Bankside. The Rose, an investment of the impresario Philip Henslowe, had been there since 1587. Four centuries later the site of the Rose was uncovered by construction workers putting up an office building. The site has not yet been fully explored, but it has emerged that the structure was a fourteen-sided polygon, the sides of irregular length. It is not certain that it had a fixed, permanent stage. The Rose is important because it was the first of the nine open-air playhouses built in Shakespeare's lifetime, and because at least two of his plays – *1 Henry VI* and *Titus Andronicus* – are known to have been staged there. Further archaeological work may yield explanations for the strange design of the Rose and its successors and competitors. (An up-to-date report on the research is provided by Andrew Gurr, 'New Questions about the Rose', *Times Literary Supplement*, 18 April 2003, pp. 14–15.)

Another playhouse, the Swan, built on the South Bank, was in operation by 1596, when a Dutch visitor, Johannes de Witt, made the celebrated sketch which is the only contemporary representation of an Elizabethan theatre complete with an actor on stage. It is the subject of much learned controversy, and Andrew Gurr puts it mildly when he remarks that it would be putting it mildly to call some of its features debatable. De Witt visited and admired the four playhouses: the Rose, the Theatre, the Curtain and the Swan. The most splendid of these were the two on the South Bank, the Rose and the Swan, especially the latter, which was, he said, the largest, with a capacity of three thousand. He particularly admired the stage pillars, painted to look like marble.

The modern replica of the Globe on Bankside, which we owe largely to the extraordinary exertions of the late Sam Wanamaker, was partly based on what was being learned about the Rose. It does not satisfy the experts on all points, but it has proved an interesting and lively playing place. It gives what seems a fair idea of the original, and offers the unfamiliar experience of audience participation, an everyday matter for the patrons at the original Globe, but lost when theatres retreated behind their proscenium arches. Of course we shall never recapture the atmosphere of those original buildings, large and splendid and decorated to the point of gaudiness, rather like the cinemas of the 1930s.

What went on behind the scenes of these remarkable Elizabethan theatres? One of the richer sources of information is the diary of Philip Henslowe, owner of the Rose and later, in 1614, of another South Bank building, the Hope, which he designed for bear-baiting as well as plays. Henslowe was not only a theatre manager but also a brothel owner, a property dealer, and a pawnbroker. Best, perhaps, to call him an entrepreneur. He managed the Rose for the Admiral's Men until compelled by the success of the nearby Globe to seek audiences elsewhere. He built another theatre called the Fortune on the north side of the river, well away from its Southwark rivals. It was rectangular rather than polygonal in design, but the builder's contract, which survives, shows that the plan was adapted from that of the Globe, acknowledged by this shrewd operator as the best model.

That was in 1600. Henslowe had dealings with other companies, and his accounts record loans and payments to playwrights, naming many plays, and they are instructive on such matters as stage properties – rocks, cages, tombs, coffins, mitres, and so on. A celebrated item was a 'robe for to go invisible'. The most valuable items were costumes: a velvet cloak embroidered with silver and gold, worn by the star actor Alleyn, cost £20 10 6d, which, as Gurr points out, was 'more than a third of Shakespeare's price for a house in Stratford'. Henslowe lists many such garments, appropriate to various ranks and vocations. In an age when the status of the wearer was signified by his or her clothes, one could not put great men and women on the stage in cheap garments.

Henslowe was the ancestor, in Shakespeare's lifetime, of the modern theatre mogul. Shakespeare and his associates, now about to compete with Henslowe in the same small area of the South Bank, were in a smaller, more specific line of business, but, as we have seen, business it was. Shakespeare's main contribution was to provide plays, which he did with obvious diligence. Other dramatists were less prudent or less committed to one company. Thomas Heywood claims to have written two hundred and twenty plays, either alone or in collaboration. Working mostly by himself, Shakespeare did not need to be so prolific. He owned a tenth of the enterprise as well as writing for it.

How he became a sharer in the first place is obscure. Perhaps the plays he brought with him to the Lord Chamberlain's Men were worth enough to buy his share; perhaps, as the story goes, Southampton gave him what he needed. Once such a tale attaches itself to Shakespeare it can hardly ever be dislodged, but Southampton had his own money troubles, and his gift is reported to have been of £1000, the equivalent of perhaps half a million in modern money. That would be an astonishing gift from a nobleman to a common player, as well as being far more than the occasion required. It is more sensible to suppose that the prudent young man had acquired the necessary sum by his own exertions.

We can be fairly sure that Shakespeare made little from the sale of his works to the printers. Eighteen of his plays were published, not always in authorized editions, during his lifetime. Although he seems to have attended carefully to the proofing of *Venus and Adonis* and *The Rape of Lucrece*, it seems clear that he took no such trouble with the plays. The posthumous Folio of 1623 includes the eighteen that were already in print and eighteen more, now printed for the first time. *Pericles* was absent, to be included in the Third Folio of 1664. Among the plays included in the canon as having the authority of Heminges and Condell, the actor friends of Shakespeare who collected the plays, is *Henry VIII* (or *All Is True*), which was almost certainly written in collaboration with John Fletcher. *The Two Noble Kinsmen*, also written with Fletcher, remained unpublished until 1634, when it announced its joint authorship on the title page; but it was not included in the Folio of 1664, nor in the Fourth, of 1685, which reprinted the Third.

After 1594 Shakespeare seems to have been almost entirely a man of the theatre. He wrote plays, one or two a year; he certainly acted in some of them, perhaps playing old men like Hamlet's father and Adam in *As You Like It*. Recent computer-aided statistical research suggests that he may also have played Aaron, the black villain of *Titus Andronicus*; Ulysses in *Troilus and Cressida*; and Desdemona's father Brabantio in

Othello. These conjectures are very uncertain, but we may take it that he achieved little celebrity as a performer in a company led by the great Burbage and boasting, in succession, two distinguished comic actors, Will Kempe and Robert Armin. No doubt Shakespeare wrote with particular members of the company in mind. It was almost certainly for Burbage that he wrote the great tragic roles – Hamlet, Othello, Macbeth, Lear, Timon, Coriolanus.

Kempe, whose roles probably included Dogberry and Bottom, sold his share and left the company on the eve of the opening of the Globe to undertake his famous morris dance to Norwich. In the book he produced to exploit that feat he found space to ridicule his ex-partners. Perhaps there had been a row about the new theatre, its design and location. In any case the other sharers acquired in Kempe's place Robert Armin, a more subtle and intelligent comedian, who was before long to play Feste in *Twelfth Night* and the Fool in *Lear*. It is fair to conjecture that if Armin had not joined the company these roles might not exist in the forms familiar to us.

Of the plays we assume Shakespeare brought with him in 1594, four are history plays and form a sequence recounting the stormy reigns of Henry VI and his usurpers up to the overthrow of Richard III at Bosworth. The second cycle followed in the later 1590s, going back in time to describe the reign and deposition of Richard II and ending with the victories of Henry V in France. This second tetralogy is of a much higher order of achievement. Shakespeare's persistence with the history play is ample proof that the genre was popular. He wrote, in addition to the eight plays mentioned above, *King John* and *Henry VIII*, and probably had a hand in an eleventh, *Edward III*; so something between a quarter and a third of his plays are about

English history. Taken all together, they cover the period between the reigns of Richard II, who died in 1399, and Elizabeth's father, Henry VIII, who died in 1547.

Only the last of these plays was written after the building of the Globe. When it was performed in 1613 there must have been members of the audience who had lived during the reign of Henry's daughter, and a few might even have lived under Henry himself, so they witnessed scenes that were both remote and close at hand. It was at a performance of *Henry VIII* in 1613 – quite possibly at the first performance – that the Globe burned down, its thatch having been set alight by the wadding of a ceremonial cannon shot. By all accounts it was a very grand production ('with many extraordinary circumstances of pomp and majesty', according to Sir Henry Wotton), and there is a mildly satisfying sense of *Götterdämmerung* about this conclusion to a series of plays that had occupied the author, on and off, for so many years.

That was the end of the Globe, or at any rate of the first Globe, for it was rebuilt on the same site. We must now consider for a moment not its end but its origin. The building and fitting out of the Globe Theatre on Bankside in 1598 was probably the most turbulent episode in the careers of a group of men quite accustomed to emergencies of one kind or another. As mentioned earlier, a dispute with the landlord had prevented their using the Theatre north of the river, and its lease was expiring; accordingly they rather daringly defied the landlord and, having dismantled the Theatre timber by timber, carried it across the Thames, using the old material to build a new playhouse – an amphitheatre like the Rose and the Swan, but the grandest of the public theatres. It must have been the most conspicuous of the various places of entertainment in Southwark, that centre of entertainment both licit and illicit.

The new theatre was legally described as 'a house newly built with a garden attached... in the occupation of William Shakespeare and others'. Performances would be in the afternoon, their imminence announced by a trumpet call from the roof. Together with the house flag (probably bearing an image of Hercules supporting his load, the world – the globe, the Globe), the trumpet summoned all within sight or hearing to come to the play (a survival, perhaps, of old touring practices). The clientele could make the short crossing of the Thames from north to south bank by wherry, or they could save the fare and walk across nearby London Bridge.

Once at the theatre you got in by paying a penny, a price that entitled you to stand in the yard. Another penny and you had access to a gallery, and for more money you could have a seat. The best people sat in the Lords' Room, which cost quite a lot more. The admission charges, somehow defying inflation, had remained constant throughout the years of metropolitan theatrical history.

The platform or main playing area extended into the yard. Behind it was the 'tiring-house', or, as we should say, the green room, with a tarras – a recessed balcony above – between it and the platform. Over the stage was a cover known as 'the heavens', decorated with stars and supported by two pillars which sometimes did duty for trees. This new stage also had a trap, and machinery for lowering objects or persons onto the stage.

A young Swiss visitor, Thomas Platter, saw *Julius Caesar* in the 'straw-thatched house' in September 1599. He liked the show and made special mention of the terminal jig: 'at the end of the play they [the actors] danced together admirably and exceedingly gracefully, according to their custom, two in each group dressed in men's and two in women's apparel.' Nobody seemed to think there was anything odd about ending a performance of a solemn play about ancient Romans in this fashion. A performance of *Hamlet* plus a dance or a jig with dialogue, sometimes bawdy, was a decent pennyworth, even if a journeyman's wage was only a shilling a day.

One must remember that the Elizabethan taste for plays was of a piece with a love for other public entertainments such as fencing, bear-baiting, and cock-fighting. There were specially designed cockpits, one of which was later converted into the Phoenix or Drury Lane Theatre, and thereafter stage plays alternated with cockfights. The Hope Theatre on Bankside, already mentioned, had been a 'bear garden' before Henslowe made it into a theatre in 1613, after which date it served both purposes. Londoners may reflect that in our own time the Albert Hall is a multi-purpose amphitheatre, used for operas, symphony concerts, boxing, tennis tournaments, and national celebrations such as Armistice Day.

But Shakespeare's Globe was a specialist theatre, and to that extent it distinguished drama from the miscellany of amusements all around it. The older, more primitive passion for performance, as in old folk entertainments such as the miracle plays and the mummers' play (remembered by Shakespeare in *Twelfth Night*), persisted, though in professional forms. We have seen that there was a strong theatrical element in society generally, as seen in the rituals of execution or in displays of royal and civic power – even in the way authority dealt with lepers. Leprosy had waned to the point of extinction by the end of the century, but as long as it was around it called for the remarkable ceremonies described in Steven Mullaney's book *The Place of the Stage* (1988). Lepers were treated as dead, having been divorced and subjected to last rites, before being shipped over to Southwark – regarded by the London authorities as a moral refuse dump – to live as they pleased. But there had to be ceremonies, enactments, first. Shows were an essential part of daily life, some solemn, some comic; a tragedy followed by a dance was nothing out of the way.

Most of the audience, then, resembled Platter in finding nothing inappropriate in that final dance (though Hamlet seems to deplore the custom when he says Polonius is 'for a jig or a tale of bawdry, or he sleeps' (II.ii.500–1). We need to think of the actors as versatile, even as athletes – tumblers, dancers, swordsmen, adaptable to all demands on them – as well as master rhetoricians. They catered to audiences that enjoyed both jigs and tragedies.

The Globe offered very sophisticated drama in a house designed to do it justice, but it never quite outgrew its origins. It abandoned the model offered by the old inn-yards that were the first theatres, but its polygonal shape mimicked that of the neighbouring bear-pits. A bear might be tormented in one while Othello was baited in another. Both were entertainments and one might be played at court, but essentially they were both for the people.

The new theatre is thought to have been large, with audiences up to two and a half or three thousand, as at the Swan. It has been estimated that in 1595 the two acting companies then at work had audiences of fifteen thousand weekly. The house might be full on public holidays, perhaps only half full on other days. Audiences would obviously be smaller in the winter months. John Webster's preface to his play *The White Devil*

(1609) complains that it was acted 'in so dull a time of winter, presented in so open and black a theatre that it wanted...a full and understanding auditory'. He goes on to condemn the ignorance and stupidity of audiences at 'that playhouse' (the Red Bull, north of the river), perhaps regretting that the play had not been done in a private theatre, indoors. But the open-air theatres did not close for winter, and the box office returns must have made it worthwhile to keep them open. (From 1609 Shakespeare's company did close the Globe in the winter months and use the Blackfriars.) The population of London was then perhaps four hundred thousand, so the attendance at theatres was impressively large.

Thomas Platter also saw a play at the Curtain, a playhouse built in 1577 in Shoreditch, north of the Thames but outside the jurisdiction of the City authorities. He made notes as follows:

> Daily at two in the afternoon London has two, sometimes three plays running at different places, competing with each other... The plays are so constructed that they play on a raised platform, so that everyone has a good view. There are different galleries and places, however, where the seating is better and more comfortable and therefore more expensive. For whoever cares to stand below pays one English penny, but if he wishes to sit he enters by another door, and pays another penny, while if he desires to sit in the more comfortable seats which are cushioned, where he not only sees everything well, but can also be seen, then he pays yet another English penny at another door. And during the performance food and drink are carried round the audience, so that for what one cares to pay one may also have refreshment.

Platter's account of the Curtain doesn't exactly match what is known of the Globe, where prices for the better parts of the auditorium were higher, but the principle would be the same. Snacks, nuts and bottled beer would be sold in both houses. Incidentally, few theatrical historians omit to remind us that these theatres had no lavatories.

The audience was obviously drawn from high and low. Those called by Gabriel Harvey 'the wiser sort' – who enjoyed *Hamlet* in the same spirit as they admired *The Rape of Lucrece*, which of course was written for the page rather than the stage – would no doubt be in the better seats. But the mass audience, while not indifferent to high rhetorical flights, also wanted blood and revenge and jokes. Jokes, if intruded by the clown, annoyed Hamlet, and perhaps also the wiser sort. Jigs and bawdry – one of the beauties of *Hamlet* was that it provided all those things while its hero condemned them, and displayed all the arts of language and personation at the same time.

Prolific though he certainly was, Shakespeare could not alone have supplied the company with all the plays they needed, and that may serve as a reminder that for all his eminence, and the relative neglect of the other dramatists of the period, he does not stand alone. Many plays that help to justify talk of the greatness of the early English theatre were written and played – most often at the Globe – during the first decade of the seventeenth century, and they were not all by Shakespeare.

Who were his rivals? Marlowe, born in 1564, the year of Shakespeare's birth, achieved fame first, but was murdered in 1593. By 1600 a generation of poet-dramatists had departed. Thomas Kyd, Marlowe's room-mate and author of *The Spanish*

Tragedy (a revenge play that started a fashion and has interesting connections with *Hamlet*), died in 1594. Robert Greene, who had notoriously sneered at the upstart Shakespeare, died in 1592. George Peele, one of the rather short-lived 'University Wits' along with Marlowe, Lyly, Greene and Nashe, died in 1597.

Among the dramatists writing in Shakespeare's heyday were Ben Jonson, John Marston, Thomas Heywood, Thomas Middleton, John Webster and George Chapman. Of these, Jonson and Chapman were the most distinguished poets outside as well as inside the theatre. Chapman was the translator of Homer ('never before in any language truly translated'). His fame now rests largely on that translation, which he himself described as 'the work that I was born to do'. He never wrote for Shakespeare's company, but his dramatic works include some strong tragedies, notably *Bussy d'Ambois* (1604), a play for St Paul's Boys (George Hunter thinks it worth remarking that this very grand and philosophical hero must have been played by a boy no older than seventeen [348]). *Bussy* was later revived by the King's Men, and Chapman wrote a sequel, *The Revenge of Bussy d'Ambois,* as well as three other tragedies based on contemporary French history. He also wrote comedies, and in 1605 collaborated with Jonson and Marston on the ill-fated *Eastward Ho!,* which made rude remarks about the Scots and earned the authors a spell in prison.

Apart from these theatrical adventures, and the great translation, Chapman wrote some very obscure poems (*The Shadow of Night,* 1594, and *Ovid's Banquet of Sense,* 1595) which were expressly intended to appeal to only a few choice spirits, expert in the darkest kind of Renaissance allegory. C. S. Lewis dismissed them because he was repelled by the parts of the poems he could understand and willing only to say that 'what remains obscure might, for all we know, have something of value'. But students of this period should not push these poems away so petulantly; allegory, sometimes very dark, is an important constituent of its poetry. Writing for a larger and less learned public, Shakespeare himself, though he knew that on the popular stage a little allegory would go a long way, made more use of it than is sometimes supposed. He practised it expertly in his great metaphysical lyric 'The Phoenix and Turtle', and occasionally in the Sonnets, though he was never as wilfully occult as Chapman, who is thought by some to be the Rival Poet of the Sonnets, commended for 'the proud full sail of his great verse'. Chapman was an intellectual in a sense that probably excludes Shakespeare; like the aristocratic poet Fulke Greville, friend and biographer of Sidney, he had a deep interest in the revived philosophy of Stoicism.

Like Chapman, Jonson on occasion wrote for Henslowe, and for the boys' companies, but also, at the other end of the social scale, for James I and Charles I, becoming a specialist in the genre of the court masque. His work for Shakespeare's company included the great comedies *Volpone* and *The Alchemist*, as well as *Bartholomew Fair* (1614), that remarkable report on London street life. Shakespeare himself makes a rare appearance as an actor in the cast list of Jonson's *Every Man in His Humour*, a satirical comedy of 1598.

Of Webster's violent Italianate tragedies *The White Devil* and *The Duchess of Malfi*, works of lofty poetic pretensions which contain many reminiscences of Shakespeare, the first failed at the down-market venue of the Red Bull in Clerkenwell, and the second was probably played by Shakespeare's company at both the Globe and the Blackfriars, a private indoor theatre of which more shall be said later. It was expensive and cannot have seated more than about six hundred, but it had the great advantage of offering cover during the London winter. It certainly did not replace the big outdoor Globe, but it sought to please a richer clientele and was to prove very profitable. It was also to have more influence on theatre design and indeed on the future of drama generally than the open-air amphitheatres.

Shakespeare's career was nearing an end by the time Webster got going, and Thomas Middleton's great plays – the tragedies *Women Beware Women* and *The Changeling*, along with the brilliant comedy *A Chaste Maid in Cheapside* and the politically sensational *A Game at Chess* – belong to the next decade or later. Meanwhile, Shakespeare's chosen successor, John Fletcher, was starting his prolific career during which he would write, alone or in collaboration, many plays for the Blackfriars as well as for the Globe. Although Shakespeare was even in his own day admired 'this side of idolatry', we need to remember that there was a unique flowering of poetry inside the theatre as well as outside. Many poets worked in both fields, resorting to the drama and the mercies of Henslowe when more respectable patronage could not be found.

Indeed Shakespeare's was an age of vast and various poetic achievement, a period unparalleled in the history of anglophone poetry. We can believe that in a London that was still, as cities go, manageable – Shakespeare could go pretty well anywhere he wanted to on foot or by a boat across the river – many of these exuberant practitioners must have known one another, the more easily if they lived in or near the theatre districts. Poets and pamphleteers, actors and musicians, could have gathered together without much effort. The old story of poets, including Shakespeare, regularly drinking together at the Mermaid tavern thus has a kind of truth, even if it never happened, at least in his day. Nor was the atmosphere continuously convivial; these men could be quarrelsome to the point of murder. The so-called War of the Poets (*Poetomachia*) and War of the Theatres (1600–2) was a significant row – a quarrel between poets that was also a conflict between different kinds of theatre and acting styles. The principal opponents were Jonson and Marston. Jonson, in his play *The Poetaster* (1601), performed by boys, ridiculed Marston for his pretentious vocabulary, while Marston and Dekker's play *Satiromastix* (1601), performed by men, sneered at Jonson's claims to be a champion of morality. The theatre world enjoyed gossiping about the dispute, as may be seen from Hamlet's comments on it when he first meets Rosencrantz and Guildenstern in the Folio version of the play (II.ii.327ff.). The row was notorious – 'there has been much throwing about of brains' (358–59), and the episode in *Poetaster* when Crispinus (Marston) is forced to take an emetic and vomit up his fancy words must have hurt him – yet Jonson collaborated with both Marston and Dekker. Theirs was a small world.

Marston is in his way a writer more representative of his period than either Chapman or Shakespeare, for Shakespeare, once established, rarely wrote anything not intended for the stage. Ten or eleven years Shakespeare's junior, Marston went on from Oxford to study law, but in his early twenties set up as an author. During the 1590s erotic poetry and satire were fashionable genres, and Marston worked with some success in both; but in 1598 the Bishop of London used his authority to suppress them, and in the following year Marston's satires were publicly burned. Jonson found ways of transferring his own satirical writing to the stage, and Marston also inevitably turned to playwriting. Most of his work after 1599 was written for boys' companies. Among his plays the best remembered are *Antonio and Mellida* (1599) and a sequel, *Antonio's Revenge* (1600), which, as G. K. Hunter puts it, deal with 'bizarre political villains...surrounded by comic toadies'. He was prolific in the first decade of the new century, and his revenge plays, roughly contemporary with *Hamlet*, have been held to have had some relation to that play, perhaps to an earlier version now lost.

Marston, then, was a writer whose work ranged over many poetic areas, but his main income was presumably from the playhouse. There were many such. There were also gentlemen who did not write for the public theatre, though they might produce 'closet drama', tragedies to be read, not acted. Samuel Daniel, a fairly exact contemporary of Shakespeare and a versatile poet, was one such; Fulke Greville, Sidney's friend, also a poet of stature, was another. Sidney, the great model of aristocratic courtesy, disliked the public theatre and said so in his *Apology for Poetry* (1583). Edmund Spenser, generally accepted as the master poet of his age, whose work is most closely associated with the cult of the Queen and her politics, did not write for the public stages. In the 1590s John Donne was writing, for private circulation, his extremely original love poems and satires. We have it on the authority of Izaak Walton that Donne, as well as being 'a great visitor of ladies', was also 'a great frequenter of plays'. He was merely the best of a crowd of gifted poets. I have said nothing of the pack of popular writers, the pamphleteers, ballad-makers, and men like Thomas Deloney, the Norwich silk-weaver who wrote short novels about weavers, shoemakers, and the like. London was a hive of authorial industry; much of the product, though by no means all of it, was bought by the theatre companies.

Given their organization – sharers and hired men – the companies were in some respects rather like the craft guilds of an earlier age, but modernized so that they also resembled City companies devoted to profit from commercial enterprises. Shakespeare's company seems to have been well run and was the most successful financially. Relations between the companies were competitive, but there must have been some degree of collaboration as well. The boys or their managers were serious rivals, but it seems that on occasion the men would hire the boys when their voices broke, and so those companies provided a kind of apprenticeship (a point Hamlet makes in the conversation with Rosencrantz and Guildenstern mentioned above).

Each company catered to its regular patrons, the Globe being up-market from the other public theatres; the difference might be compared to that between a broadsheet and a tabloid newspaper. The Red Bull favoured the sensational, but the Globe did not exactly struggle to avoid it, for its patrons obviously enjoyed revenge and the tragedy of blood. Shakespeare never wrote for the Globe anything quite like his early *Titus*, but *Hamlet*, which had begun life in the late 1580s in a version now lost, records the death by one means or another of almost the entire cast. Like Kyd's *Spanish Tragedy* (improved by additions from Jonson's hand), *Titus* was still being performed in 1614, when Jonson deplored its popularity in the Introduction to *Bartholomew Fair*. The subtleties of *The Tempest* did not drive from the stage the simplicities of the early romance *Mucedorus*, which was constantly reprinted and performed. It seems that the simpler types of play – romance or revenge –

continued to appeal to the audiences of the new century, while the playwrights tested those audiences, or some of them, with far more taxing material, replete with complicated variations and psychological subtleties. Such was the relationship of old to new. In fact old and new were not all that far apart in time – there were only a dozen years or so between the old and the new *Hamlet*. Hamlet himself is aware of this when he converses with the itinerant players and remembers the ranting vein of the old tragedies.

The acting style of the Globe was markedly different, much as the style of *Hamlet* generally differs from that of the specimen speech of Hamlet's actor. There has been much learned dispute about acting styles in Shakespeare's theatre, but it is surely clear that they changed considerably in the course of his career, as Hamlet, in his discourse on the subject, seems to suggest:

> Speak the speech, I pray you, as I pronounc'd it, trippingly on the tongue, but if you mouth it, as many of our players do, I had as lief the town-crier spoke my lines. Nor do not saw the air too much with your hand, thus, but use all gently, for in the very torrent, tempest, and, as I may say, whirlwind of your passion, you must acquire and beget a temperance that may give it smoothness… Suit the action to the word, the word to the action, with this special observance. That you o'erstep not the modesty of nature: for anything so o'erdone is from the purpose of playing.
>
> (III.ii.1–20)

Though the character of the productions of the highly professional boys' companies must remain obscure to us, we can guess that they had their roots in the academic tradition, long established in the schools and in the universities, and regarded as having an educational purpose. Their acting style might therefore be related to the rhetoric in which pupils were instructed – a mode of discourse based on established rules concerning elocution and gesture. But of course the boys acted indoors, which flattered their vocal powers. The rival tradition, going back to the days of vagrant entertainers and impromptu performances, had its own version of rhetoric and its own temptations to rant, to out-Herod the Herod of the miracle plays; and in any case it would be wrong to insist too strongly on the difference between the traditions, for the public drama-tists had also studied rhetoric and practised the arts of decla-mation at grammar school (Stratford Grammar School, for instance) or university. Marlowe's verse is highly rhetorical, and so is that of the early Shakespeare. Nor should we expect that the degree of naturalism apparently recommended by Hamlet would entirely exclude these rhetorical traits; indeed, they persist in modified forms on the modern stage. But once again *Hamlet* instructs us. When the hero is ranting, as in the quarrel with Laertes over Ophelia's grave, he is very conscious that he is doing so:

> And if thou prate of mountains, let them throw
> Millions of acres on us, till our ground,
> Singeing his pate against the burning zone,
> Make Ossa like a wart! Nay, and thou'lt mouth,
> I'll rant as well as thou.
>
> (V.i.280–4)

In *Hamlet* our attention is inescapably drawn to such ironic manipulations of register; witness the language of the actor's specimen speech and the verse of the play-within-the-play – 'The Mousetrap' is given a different dialect, an older dramatic style, calling for extravagant speech and gesture and clearly marked off from the verse in the play proper. By the time of *Hamlet*, and indeed earlier – in *Romeo and Juliet* and, in a perfectly distinct manner, *Julius Caesar* – the technique of characterization is so developed that much more variety of tone is required than in earlier tragedy. The blank verse is looser, there is more scope for interpretation; and the verse that makes such feats possible distances itself from all earlier styles. Acting moved away from oratory. As Andrew Gurr puts it,

> That the academic term 'acting' should become so completely the prerogative of the common players as it did in the early seventeenth century is the most striking testimony to their predominance over the orators. More significantly, perhaps, what the players were presenting on the stage at the beginning of the century was distinctive enough to require a whole new term to describe it.

The term, referred to above, was 'personation'. It meant that the actors were liberated by this new dramatic language to explore the minds of the characters they represented. A new manner of great acting had been created.

In *Coriolanus* the hero's mother, Volumnia, remarks that 'Action is eloquence, and the eyes of th' ignorant / More learned than their ears' (III.ii.76–7); and it was sometimes stated that one could guess the sense of an oration when too far off to hear it by observing the gestures of the speaker. Volumnia is referring to orators, not actors – perhaps she has in mind a preacher addressing a large audience, as might happen, for instance, at St Paul's, rather than a player on the stage – or, if indeed she had the theatre in mind, then of an older style closer to the academic, perhaps even that of a boy actor.

Shakespeare had reason not to like the boys' companies, for they were 'most tyrannically clapp'd' (*Hamlet* II.ii.340–1) and their success had compelled professional men to tour. Moreover the boys had *Poetaster*, and Shakespeare's company had *Satiromastix*. Possibly the Globe style did not suit more old-fashioned patrons, at any rate at first. Hamlet remarks with some irony that when the boys' voices broke they might become 'common players' and therefore Shakespeare's employees – the more reason why they should not now 'exclaim against their own succession' (II.ii.351). They will then have to learn a new craft. The differences between boys and men must have been very obvious, and part of the business of competition; for the time being, however, the adult companies and their acting style would recover and prevail.

So the move to the Globe may be thought a moment of great importance in Shakespeare's career. Surrounded by players of talent, he was embarking on his most fruitful decade. Despite many guesses, we know little about his private life at that time except that he must have been secure financially and keen to remain so. Not much can be said about his visits to Stratford, where he had a wife and children. In 1596 he lost his son Hamnet (the name is a variant of Hamlet), born in 1585, but Hamnet's twin Judith survived, and so did Susanna (born in 1583). They cannot have seen very much of Shakespeare. William's father, who had assiduously acquired property in Stratford before falling on hard times, died aged about seventy, in 1601. We have seen that his religious adherence has caused much speculation about his son's, and there has been more speculation about the effect of his death, and Hamnet's, on the work of William; but in such cases proofs are usually hard to adduce.

In 1597, just before he acquired his ten per cent share of the Globe profits, the playwright bought New Place, the second largest house in Stratford, and in 1601 he inherited two more houses, his father's property in Henley Street. He engaged in other business transactions – purchases of land and tithes – and was further enriched by the eventual success of the company in the Blackfriars. As late as 1613, three years before his death, he bought a small house in the Blackfriars precinct. Perhaps, as most biographers believe, he meant to retire to Stratford; he certainly retained an interest in his property there and thereabouts, and died there in 1616. And possibly the newly acquired London house was an investment intended to produce rent; but one wonders whether he did not continue to spend much time in the city. The house was practically next door to the theatre, very convenient for a man working there daily. His plays were still being performed, and in 1613 he was still writing for the company, though probably only as a collaborator. The journey to and from Stratford was surely too long and weary, the roads too terrible for much of the year, to encourage regular commuting.

Still, he seems to have kept up his connection with his home town more consistently than many who flee from the provinces to the metropolis. However commercial and litigious the records may seem, Shakespeare was an eminent citizen of Stratford who, like so many, had journeyed to London to make his fortune. If England has a heart, Stratford is close to it. Nearby Warwick and Coventry offered the experience of quite large towns and might whet the appetite for greater adventures. London was at least accessible. Shakespeare was lucky; poets born in Carlisle or Newcastle could hardly have led a double life in city and country even to the extent of Shakespeare's. Poets born in London, like Ben Jonson, had to make do with the country round London (still, it must be said, easy to get to), and Jonson also explored the country on foot, making his celebrated walk to Edinburgh; it is still remembered in Newcastle that he bought a new pair of boots there on his way. Shakespeare seems to have undertaken no such splendid feats; he preferred horses, and the miry road from Stratford via Oxford.

8   Plays at the Globe

We may guess that *As You Like It*, dated 1599, was an early Globe play. The dancing clown Will Kempe had just left the company, and Touchstone must have been written for Robert Armin, subtler and wittier, later the Fool in *Lear*, while Kempe went off on that spectacular dance to Norwich – a stunt Anthony Holden compares with the modern sponsored walks undertaken by the likes of the cricketer Ian Botham, though Kempe kept the proceeds. (Ben Jonson was another contender for the crown of spectacular walks.) Holden also remarks, justly, that *As You Like It* is 'riddled with theatrical self-reference, as if the entire company was ... excited about its new theatre'. In this it resembles *Hamlet*, a play performed perhaps a year later. *As You Like It* is as sophisticated as the comedies that preceded it, and some of its effect depends on the audience's knowing something about the vogue for pastoral poetry in Elizabeth's later years. Pastoral depends on the contrast of manners (and honesty) between court and country. What the courtiers experience when they leave the court is a range of pastoral attitudes, from the primitive virtue of old Adam to the dullness of William and the ornamental relationship of Phebe and Silvius. Satirical comment is accompanied by courtly melancholy; Touchstone is a court clown and Jaques an urban satirist of a kind that flourished in the 1590s until satire was banned. Rosalind commands the scene with her superior rank and wit. The rustics are sometimes mocked and sometimes teased and exploited. There is an expressed willingness to endure the hard life in the forest, the benign though bitter aspect of nature missing from many pastorals; but the court personages are still glad to go back to where they belong, presumably the wiser for the experience, and ready to run the world again.

The contrasts presented are traditional: court and country, action and contemplation. Rosalind is one of Shakespeare's witty, sensible, outspoken, and well-born women; some may think there is too much of her chatter, but hers is a memorable trouser role, and once again one marvels at the versatility of the boy actors who played not only Rosalind and Beatrice but also (probably in their later adolescence) Lady Macbeth, Cleopatra and Hermione in *The Winter's Tale*. (It is said that some boys went on playing female roles till they were as old as eighteen.) The play is rich and allusive, even to modern ears, and it must have meant much more to a contemporary audience.

Henry V makes what seem like obvious references to the new theatre (though most of the Prologue's remarks would apply to any theatre) and it does so with a kind of mock modesty, deprecating its glorious name, since it cannot be truly an image of the whole world. 'But pardon, gentles all, / The flat unraised spirits that hath dar'd / On this unworthy scaffold to bring forth / So great an object' (Prologue) and 'Be kind, / And eke out our performance with your mind' (III *Chorus* 34–5). Yet there is a certain exultation in these choruses, as if the new theatre, for all its grandeur, had prompted such reflections. The theatre's flag showed Hercules holding up the globe of the world, a feat which, in a sense, was what the actors were emulating; the very modesty of the disavowals draws attention to the presumptuousness of the boast.

Henry V was the last of the histories except for *Henry VIII*, a good many years later; and one thinks of Shakespeare at the Globe as primarily a writer of tragedy. *Julius Caesar* was certainly played there, for the Swiss Thomas Platter records his attendance on 21 September 1599. Elizabethans had a great interest in Roman history, especially from the time of Caesar's assassination in 44 BC to the victory of Octavius, the future Emperor Augustus, at Actium in 31 BC. The death of Caesar (though a kind of regicide) opened the road to empire, and the Roman Empire would be Christianized by Constantine in the fourth century AD. Britain had been part of the Roman Empire and the propagandists liked to suggest that there was a direct link between Constantine, born in York of an English mother, and the present empress. Moreover, Julius Caesar was known to have set foot on her shores, so plays about him were not rare, and might be seen as having relevance to modern England. Brutus was a regicide to royalists but a hero to republicans, as he was, for instance, to Michelangelo. The notion of a republic was strange, though not without interest, to Englishmen, who knew something about the constitution of Venice. The question, was it right to kill a tyrant, was answered positively by some enemies of the Crown. But was Caesar a tyrant in fact or only potentially, as Brutus concedes? All the elements of political strife are present in the narrative – the mob, potentially menacing; the dictator, potentially tyrannical. In this sense *Julius Caesar* is a history play, though Shakespeare avoids some issues, for example by excluding reference to some of Caesar's incriminating acts (such as crossing the Rubicon). His Romans are not simple political types. The Mark Antony of this play is a ruthless politician but also a very ample sketch of the older man, the lover of Cleopatra, who failed in the end to take over and orientalize the Roman Empire. Octavius has an important political role, but is beautifully rendered as the cold, graceless conqueror whose prime victim will be Cleopatra; yet *Julius Caesar* makes nothing, directly, of the historical fact that the young soldier would become the first emperor, Augustus. That transformation was reserved for the more expansive and political *Antony and Cleopatra*.

The main source of *Julius Caesar* is Plutarch in his *Lives* of Caesar, Brutus and Antony. Plutarch, though much admired in Shakespeare's day, was a republican, and so rather distant in sentiment from most Elizabethans, who were inclined to agree that monarchy was the best form of government; and Shakespeare read him in an English translation of a French translation of the Greek original, which imposed a little more distance. He handles his source with his usual freedom, but often stays quite close to North's translation, as he does in the later Roman plays. He is generous to Brutus, omitting some rather sleazy aspects of his career and emphasizing the purity of his motives compared with those of Cassius. Brutus is a tyrannicide, but the motives expressed in his soliloquy (II.i.10–34) are mixed and obscure; as Coleridge pointed out, there were ample proofs of Caesar's ambition that Brutus ignores, and he seems to produce no very strong reason for joining the conspiracy. Shakespeare's real interest in this character may be found in the brief passage a little later in the same scene:

> Since Cassius first did whet me against Caesar,
> I have not slept.
> Between the acting of a dreadful thing
> And the first motion, all the interim is

> Like a phantasma or a hideous dream.
> The Genius and the mortal instruments
> Are then in council; and the state of a man,
> Like to a little kingdom, suffers then
> The nature of an insurrection.
>
> (II.i.61–9)

Here we have the theme and the mood appropriate to terrible decisions, set forth fully in the opening passages of *Macbeth* but also relevant to *Hamlet*. Brutus interested Shakespeare as a man committing himself to a fatal choice, with the consequences of frustration by the Machiavellian Antony, and a noble but hopeless death.

Shakespeare makes Caesar a calm braggart, as well as stressing such infirmities as epilepsy and deafness to make it clear that the imperial boasting was rather hollow. He refers to himself in the third person (Terence Spencer pointed out that every Elizabethan schoolboy was aware that Caesar did so throughout his *Gallic Wars*, but the object here is to stress his habit of setting himself above ordinary people who have to say 'I'). Ben Jonson accused Shakespeare of writing the 'ridiculous' line 'Caesar did never wrong but with just cause', but he may have been misquoting the original ('Know, Caesar doth not wrong, nor without cause / Will he be satisfied' [III.i.47–8]); in any case, if Shakespeare was guilty he managed to eliminate the mistake.

The play has a few celebrated anachronisms, like the striking clock (II.i.191), but compared with, say, *Titus Andronicus* it impresses the modern reader as closer to history – that is, to our idea of that history. The principal characters are distanced by a prevailing solemnity of speech, a *gravitas* appropriate despite their evident human faults. One result of this careful limitation is an unusual lack of variety in the verse, as if the important thing was to make everybody sound very Roman, like senators preparing to sit for statues of themselves.

The Globe staged plays of many kinds. We cannot know the entire repertoire, but it did include Ben Jonson's learned Roman tragedies *Sejanus* and *Catiline, His Conspiracy* (1611), serious political plays but not great successes. *Sejanus* got Jonson into trouble with the censor and he was brought before the Privy Council to answer for his indiscretions. Shakespeare may have edited the text, and he certainly acted in the play, but here as a few years earlier after the rogue performance of *Richard II* he escaped censure. Unlike Jonson, he kept out of trouble. Yet Jonson's play stuck pedantically to its Latin sources, and when printed bore marginal references to validate what the actors were saying – a more scholarly procedure than using a translation of a translation of Plutarch, a writer already distant from the events he described. Jonson had more learning, Shakespeare more luck. He shared Plutarch's concern with the faults and virtues of individuals. Hence the fame of the quarrel scene between Brutus and Cassius (IV.ii), enthusiastically commended by Leonard Digges in 1640 ('how the audience / Were ravished, with what wonder went they thence') and still a favourite of amateur players and audiences well into the twentieth century.

Julius Caesar, though, in its way an experimental tragedy, deliberately using a narrow range of tones, lacked the bravura of *Romeo and Juliet* and the scope and power of the next tragedy, *Hamlet*. With that play we may think the British theatre reached its apogee; and, despite the achievements that were to follow, it is the masterpiece we associate most closely with the Globe and with the unmatched dramatic riches of the first decade of the new century.

The old play from which Shakespeare's was developed survives only as the title it has been given, the *ur-Hamlet*. It was a regular part of the job of the company playwright to refurbish old plays; this one belonged to the mid-1580s and was contemporary with Kyd's *The Spanish Tragedy*, in which a crazy father avenges the death of his son. (It is a question which of the two plays began the continuing fashion for slightly or very mad revengers; the answer depends on knowing which came first, and my choice is the old *Hamlet*, since a father avenging his son strikes me as the secondary situation; the son avenging the father must surely have come first. But the argument will continue.)

Shakespeare's revision of the old *Hamlet* must have been on the grandest scale; it is as if he used the old version as a basis for a vast experiment, bringing about a transformation equal to that which he was to effect in his work on the old *King Leir*, which, since that old play survives, we do not have to guess at. He seems to have decided to explore, regardless of the length of the product, all the possibilities inherent in the old story, and to do so with a dramaturgical and rhetorical range hugely increased by the developments of the fifteen or so years that had elapsed since the old play had had its moment.

Indeed, the length of the play is still something of a puzzle. *Othello* and *Lear* are also much longer than the average play of the time, and all three are almost twice as long as *Macbeth*. Private performance might allow of their being done at full length, but to stage an uncut *Hamlet* at the Globe, in either of the substantive texts, would have been a serious problem. Even at the fast rate of twenty lines a minute, and without intermissions, *Hamlet* would run for three and a half hours. The Folio version (likely to be more closely related to the performing text than the Quarto) saves only about 150 lines, and actually adds material, so these were not changes made in the interest of shortening the performance. The last of the soliloquies ('How all occasions do inform against me') was apparently cut, but the episode in which Rosencrantz and Guildenstern tell Hamlet about the London theatre wars was added. Of course there could have been cuts for which no evidence remains, for plays had to be adaptable to the circumstances of production. But on an afternoon in December or January, with dark coming on at four o'clock, in a theatre with no lighting, the play must have been got through in little more than two hours. The so-called 'Bad' Quarto of 1603 is a memorial reconstruction of the play (assembled, that is, from what actors remembered of their parts and the parts of other actors), perhaps as cut and patched for provincial touring; it is only half as long as the authentic versions and is largely inaccurate, especially when the reporters are trying to re-create other parts than their own. Of course the length is immaterial for readers, and there was a 'Good' Quarto published in 1604–5.

If we had to guess why the play was so long we might suggest that it was intended as a showpiece, a demonstration of the scope and powers of the company in its new theatre. The opening passages are rightly admired. Instead of telling the audience what has gone before and setting the story in action, these lines suggest darkness and cold, fear and apprehension, with alternations of rapid with stately speech. The entry of the Ghost is predicted, doubted, delayed, until it unexpectedly interrupts Bernardo's account of its previous appearance; so it manages to be both expected and unexpected. Hamlet himself is kept off the stage for a teasingly long time (170 lines), and even then we see him in the company of his mother and stepfather, and hear him soliloquize, before he arrives on the battlements. Only then, and not immediately, does he have his encounter with the Ghost, the mainspring of the plot. Deliberate deviousness then culminates in sudden, slightly crazed confrontations. No sooner is the revenge plot under way than we have the long, wilfully extended diversion of the scenes between Laertes, Ophelia and Polonius. Tension, having been created, is slackened, then pulled tighter. These dynamic variations in the plotting are echoed in the language of the play, whether in verse or prose; its virtuosity of rhythm and vocabulary are very distant from the simpler devices of *Julius Caesar*. *Romeo and Juliet* is notable for its controlled variations of manner, but it is simple compared to *Hamlet*.

Beneath all this variety of style there is a disquieting insistence on familial and other doubles. To Hamlet it is horrible that Claudius should be both uncle and father and he himself cousin and son; it is detestable that his mother and stepfather should be one flesh, that their adultery is indeed incest. The language of the play is full of linguistic doubling and uses the figure of hendiadys to an unprecedented extent ('one through two' – 'a single complex idea is expressed by two words connected by a conjunction; e.g. by two substantives with *and* instead of an adjective and a substantive' [*OED*]). The Dictionary gives an example from *Hamlet*: 'Well ratified by law and heraldry' (I.i.87), where 'law and heraldry' means 'heraldic law'; but there are many more, spread among the characters, sometimes trivial (the device is used to stress the pompousness of Polonius) and sometimes loaded with meaning. Laertes gives his sister double counsel, sometimes in hendiadys, sometimes simpler: 'the shot and danger of desire', 'the morn and liquid dew of youth', 'the perfume and suppliance of a minute' – which means something like 'a pleasant but transitory amusement', but the two nouns are interlocked and cannot be separated without loss of sense (I.iii.5ff.). Hendiadys is only the extreme form of the doubling that goes on at an extraordinary rate. No other play uses the trick so often, and some don't use it at all. The next on the list as to frequency is *Othello*, another play about adultery and improper doubling: 'the beast with two backs', which might be thought an impropriety corresponding to hendiadys.

The play itself is doubled and redoubled: Hamlet the revenger has partial doubles in Laertes and Fortinbras; Cornelius has an identical double in Voltemand, and Rosencrantz in Guildenstern. The story of the Polonius family makes for leisurely double plotting. The play-within-the-play is a double of the main action, and the Dumb Show is a double of 'the Mousetrap'. Those who act must also suffer, which is a doubling understood by everybody. Playing is a double of reality, and the Globe Theatre is a double of what Prospero calls 'the great globe itself' (*The Tempest* IV.i.153). And all this doubling took time, which is why this is the longest as well as the most remarkable of Shakespeare's plays. Its complexity and scope pay spectacular tribute to the Elizabethan audience.

During the next few years at the Globe, Shakespeare seems to have continued to exercise himself and his colleagues on unusual and difficult subjects. It is possible that *Othello* followed shortly after *Hamlet*, but the orthodox chronology places it in 1603 or 1604. If that is right, he took leave of absence from tragedy for three or four years. *Twelfth Night* was played at the Middle Temple in 1602, but that may not have been the first performance. *Troilus and Cressida* was certainly in existence by early 1603, for there is record of some complicated manoeuvres by prospective publishers. It is in some respects linguistically the most difficult of the plays, and it is often suggested that it must have been written for a special audience, probably the lawyers of the Inns of Court. The closely related pair *All's Well That Ends Well* and *Measure for Measure* are dated (more certainly in the case of the second) circa 1603-4.

It sounds like a busy schedule, but Shakespeare was, in the years under discussion, also writing some poetry other than plays. As I have already remarked, there was nothing unusual about doing so; a poet's business was to write verse, and there might be occasions when non-dramatic verse was called for. The date of the Sonnets is much disputed, and so is the order in which they should appear. But we know he was writing sonnets before 1598, during a decade when this was a popular genre, although the volume containing them did not appear until 1609. The long poem 'A Lover's Complaint', which was published with the Sonnets, is now generally taken to be by Shakespeare; if so, it was probably written in the early years of the new century, perhaps roughly at the same time as *Othello* and *Measure for Measure*. There were breaks in performance caused by plague in 1603-4 and 1606-9. It may be that the later sonnets (after number 107) were also written at that time. And some time about then Shakespeare wrote 'The Phoenix and Turtle', a poem so remarkable that despite our inherited conviction of his myriad-mindedness it still seems

PLAYS AT THE GLOBE

surprising to find it among Shakespeare's works. There is
nothing like it in the canon, and it is hard to think of any contemporary work that resembles it; possibly one could point to
Donne's 'The Ecstasy', although, difficult as it is, Donne's
poem proceeds by strenuous and continuous argument rather
than epigrammatic intensity like Shakespeare's. His is a meditation less on married love than on the paradox of union and
separation; the phoenix and the turtle are also, in a most pure
and intimate fashion, doubles:

> Property was thus appalled,
> That the self was not the same;
> Single nature's double name
> Neither two nor one was called.
>
> Reason, in itself confounded,
> Saw division grow together,
> To themselves yet neither either,
> Simple were so well compounded.

The personified 'Property' means the force that makes or pre-
serves each thing as itself, as in the general conditions of life;
here the division that normally obtains is annulled, and two
selves normally separate are now not divided. The word 'self-
same', used elsewhere by Shakespeare in a quite ordinary way
(e.g. *King Lear* II.ii.138 and a good many other places), is here
split into its components, becoming itself an image of the division of property; so, too, 'either' and 'neither', which are oppo-
sites, are compounded into a rhyme. It is possible to think of
this poem, which was written for a collection by Robert
Chester and published in 1601, as contemporary with *Hamlet*
and also with *Twelfth Night* – testimony to the great range of

tone and effect available to the poet in this, his prime; and to add the consideration that both plays, the tragedy and the comedy, concern themselves with doubles, true or illusory, and with 'property' in this special, limited sense. One already knew something about the range of the poet from the verbal fireworks of *Love's Labour's Lost*, the complex argumentation of *Troilus and Cressida*, and the famous simplicities of *Lear*; but the Sonnets are still astonishing, and so is this unique brief elegy. It does no harm to remind ourselves that Shakespeare was a contemporary and perhaps an acquaintance of Donne, who was described by Ben Jonson as 'the first poet in the world in some things', for Donne's passionate intelligence could also be bawdy or solemn, difficult or simple, and capable of astonishing in any of these moods. And he loved the theatre but did not write for it, any more than he consented to publish his poems. Later he became a famous preacher, when sermons could be witty as well as long and called for an art that might be called a cousin of the art of acting. He was a theologian and would have understood 'The Phoenix and Turtle' better than most.

The trio of plays next after *Hamlet* are often called 'Problem Plays'. The label is partly justified by the bearing each has on certain contemporary intellectual and social issues, *All's Well* being the least interesting in this respect. *Troilus and Cressida* is unique in that it sets against a deliberately debased version of the Troy story a set of debates on questions of honour, truth and value. It stands at a great distance from Homer, who knew nothing of Cressida – a medieval import whose name alone is related to that of Chryseis, a Trojan woman captured by the Greeks who was the indirect cause of the quarrel between

Achilles and Agamemnon and of Achilles's withdrawal from the fighting. It is sometimes argued that this withdrawal mirrored that of the Earl of Essex, who left the court sulking in 1598. Homer would not have involved Achilles in philosophical discussions about time with Ulysses, who is in any case using this kind of talk to get his way. He writes of no love affair between Troilus (a minor character) and Cressida. Shakespeare may have used Chapman's translation of seven books of the *Iliad,* published in 1598, but behind the play there stands a long tradition of poems and histories of the Trojan War, a tradition that notably includes Chaucer's verse novel *Troilus and Criseyde.* In any case Shakespeare uses the story for his own purposes.

Is the value of an object – a soldier, a woman, a jewel – merely the value others attribute to it? Do honour, fame, military virtue, exist only in the mouths of others? What of Helen, reputed the most beautiful of all women? Taken by the Trojans in revenge for the abduction of Hesione, was she worth a long war and so much bloodshed? Hector thinks not, and wants to let Helen go back to her husband Menelaus and bring an end to the war. He thinks value is intrinsic, and argues that Helen is destitute of the quality. But Troilus, with the support of Helen's new husband Paris, insists that value depends entirely on valuation; they took Helen for what she seemed to be, and must keep her for the sake of their own honour.

'What's aught but as 'tis valued?' he asks, and Hector replies, 'But value dwells not in particular will, / It holds his estimate and dignity / As well wherein 'tis precious of itself / As in the prizer' (II.ii.52–6). The arguments are rather abstract: is value a matter of truth or of opinion? The relation between truth and opinion had been disputed ever since Plato, but it was always recurring urgently in one form or another; opinion is lower than truth, even if it seems on occasion to coincide with it. Hector dismisses Troilus's arguments as immature, but yields to him (after all, the war couldn't stop then and there; it went on for three more years). Hector and Achilles die; Troilus, who valued Cressida by the intensity of his sensual attraction to her, is forced to watch her betray him with Diomed. (She was a byword for faithlessness, which adds obvious irony to the language of Pandarus as he sees the couple off to bed in III.ii.)

The attempt of Ulysses to lure Achilles back into the fighting is a masterly treatment of the problem of fame. Honour, fame, are merely reputation – valour as reflected back from the opinion of others; once the mirroring stops, honour fades; it is not intrinsic to its possessor but subject to the rule of time:

> Time hath, my lord, a wallet at his back,
> Wherein he puts alms for oblivion,
> A great-siz'd monster of ingratitudes.
> Those scraps are good deeds past, which are devour'd
> As fast as they are made, forgot as soon
> As done. Perseverance, dear my lord,
> Keeps honour bright...
>   Let not virtue seek
> Remuneration for the thing it was:
> For beauty, wit,
> High birth, vigour of bone, desert in service,
> Love, friendship, charity, are subjects all
> To envious and calumniating Time...
>
> (III.iii.145–74)

This is blank verse of a high order, spoken by a machiavellian

Ulysses who cares little for the sentiments he is expressing except in so far as they can tempt Achilles back. It is part of the mood of this extraordinary play that the attempt fails, just as Ulysses's earlier oration to the Greek princes (I.iii) on the divinely ordained propriety of obedience and discipline had failed to convert them to the maintenance of sound hierarchical behaviour.

The presence of complex debate has been part of the reason why this play is thought by many critics to have been written for a special audience, perhaps at one of the Inns of Court, where the arguments would be best appreciated; but it was probably performed at the Globe as well. There is no reason to suppose that an experienced audience, tutored in virtuoso dialogue by *Hamlet*, would not have enjoyed talk about the 'moral laws / Of nature and of nations' (II.ii.184–5), which Hector takes to be in accordance with reason, while Troilus's arguments show that his passions have subverted his reason. Yet, since we are as we are, the salacity of Pandarus as he procures Cressida for Troilus is more instantly attractive, for it is as sexy as anything in the canon. No doubt the parallel between Achilles and Essex would be spotted, and there might well have been more such contemporary allusions. The Elizabethan aristocracy fostered a cult of honour, and the reverse side of it was the misanthropic rant of Thersites, to whom love is lust, the quest for honour mere anger. These matters are not settled in the play; Hector and Troilus end it in death and wretchedness, and the scene in which Thersites, Ulysses and Troilus observe Cressida with Diomed (V.ii) is one of Shakespeare's most painful. Yet the great debate between the brothers holds the intellectual key to the play, and its effect is heightened by the skill of the characterization: Hector thoughtful, mature, patient, fearful of disaster; Troilus young, passionate about sex and fighting, love and honour. It is remarkable that this play was long out of favour: it returned to the stage only quite recently, though with much success.

Measure for Measure is a tragedy converted to comedy by the use of the bed-trick, one woman substituting in bed for another. Shakespeare had just used it in the inferior *All's Well* and now adapted it for use in the more serious play. Fanciful though the denouement certainly is, the central problem of the play is not a matter of folktale but something that can occur in various forms and various walks of life. It is set in Vienna, but Vienna is a surrogate for London, and the inns and brothels of the low-life scenes belong to Southwark, right next to the theatre. Questions concerning judgement and punishment must have troubled the minds of petty criminals as well as those of gentlefolk. The first words of the Duke – 'Of government the properties to unfold' (I.i.3) – sound like the opening of a verse treatise (*De Legibus...*) or of an epic poem ('Of man's first disobedience...'). The properties were Justice and Mercy, as the Duke makes clear when he delegates his authority to Angelo: 'Mortality and mercy in Vienna / Live in thy tongue and heart' (I.i.44–5).

The balance between these properties had recently (in 1596) been the subject of Book V, the Book of Justice, of Spenser's *Faerie Queene*, where in one canto the poet deals with a particularly hard case, Elizabeth's condemnation of her cousin Mary, Queen of Scots. Hard cases traditionally make bad law, and in *Measure for Measure* an especially hard case is presented as an instance of the difficult balance between the just and the unjust exercise of judicial authority. In the sixteenth century, justice was enforced in ways that now seem unjust and brutal.

Interrogation under torture, on the rack, could be guaranteed to extort false confessions. The poor crook and the whore suffered under the whip and, for quite trivial crimes, on the gallows; the aristocrats might hope to be sent to the block, rather than pressed to death, or brought to Tyburn to be torn to pieces before a gaping crowd, which was the fate of the Jesuit missionaries when caught by infamous investigators or 'pursuivants' like Topcliffe, who was allowed to keep a rack in his own house and sent many to Tyburn. Topcliffe's copy of a history of the Jesuit mission survives, with his gloating marginalia: beside the name of a missionary the words 'I racked him', beside the name of someone hanged a little stick figure dangling from a gallows. Monstrous reprisals were thought to be deterrent, an argument the Queen seems to have accepted, though she was not herself a particularly vindictive or sadistic woman.

The state enforced various sumptuary laws concerning, for instance, Lenten fasting. Citizens could have been in little doubt as to the power of Authority, which could be capricious and random; yet they may well have had it in mind that those who wielded it were themselves fallible men. The arbitrariness and cruelty of power were points that exercised the mind of Lear in his dotage. In an age when the Bible was read – when all were urged to read it – the words of St Paul would be present to many memories: 'Therefore thou art inexcusable, O man, whosoever thou art, that judgest; for wherein thou judgest another, thou damnest thyself, for thou that judgest doest the same things... And thinkest thou this, O man, that judgest them that do such things, and doest the same, that thou shalt escape the judgement of God?' (Romans 2:1–3).

Angelo's first case (he declines to judge the case of Pompey) shows that his interpretation of the Duke's orders is to be very severe; he revives an almost forgotten statute that demands the death penalty for fornication, insisting that in the present condition of the city it is an essential deterrent. Himself moved to lust by Isabella in her novice's habit, he is himself apparently guilty of the same offence when he sleeps with her, as he supposes; in fact it is with a substitute. The position is complicated by the consideration that Claudio would not have been guilty under the law of England; he can claim to have made a 'true contract' with Julietta (I.ii.145), a contract of the kind known as *sponsalia de praesenti*, effected in the presence of witnesses; though frowned upon as not consecrated in church, it was nevertheless legally binding. Claudio gives reasons why the marriage was kept secret until that was no longer possible, but insists that both parties had consented, their love being 'most mutual' (I.ii.154). The contract was lawful and irrevocable, unlike the one Angelo had formerly made with Mariana, which was *de futuro:* either party could withdraw up to the point when the union was consummated, and Angelo withdrew when Mariana lost her fortune. He consummated the marriage without knowing it when Mariana took Isabella's place in his bed, and she was thenceforth legally his wife.

Only on a severely ecclesiastical view could Claudio's marriage be called invalid, and he admits this even as he laments it, accusing himself of 'too much liberty' (I.ii.125), which is exactly what Angelo believes to be the cause of the corruption of the city. As he will shortly discover for himself, sexual desire is a powerful and destructive force: 'Our natures do pursue, / Like rats that ravin down their proper bane, / A thirsty evil, and when we drink we die' (I.ii.128–30). Claudio acknowledges Authority as the proper counter-force to desire, even as he deplores its effect on himself:

Thus can the demigod, Authority,
Make us pay down for our offence by weight –
The word of heaven – on whom it will, it will;
On whom it will not, so: yet still 'tis just.

(I.ii.120–3)

He reluctantly agrees with Angelo's remark that worse crimes go unpunished: 'I not deny / The jury, passing on the prisoner's life, / May in the sworn twelve have a thief or two, / Guiltier than him they try' (II.i.18–21). It does not follow that the lesser fault should escape.

The play puts the case for Justice as well as the case for Mercy, and it does so with great power in the scenes in which Isabella pleads with Angelo. When prayer fails to curb his desire for Isabella, Angelo has a soliloquy worthy of Hamlet (II.iv.1–17): 'Heaven in my mouth / As if I did but only chew his name', where the original text, written before the statute of 1606 forbidding mention of God's name on the stage, probably read 'God in my mouth', a black parody of the Eucharist. Equally powerful are Isabella's condemnation of Angelo's treacherous abuse of his authority (II.ii), the Duke's consolation speech to Claudio ('Be absolute for death' [III.i.5ff.]), and Claudio's agonized lapse into terror at the prospect ('Ay, but to die, and go we know not where…' [III.i.117ff.]). Few speeches in Shakespeare have such agitated power.

The setting enforces the theme. The character of Lucio, lecherous, witty, selfish, a rake, who nevertheless feels reverence for Julietta's condition; the bawds and executioners, the prison, with suggestions that would be filled out by an audience that knew about the horror and filth of Elizabethan jails – all this makes the first half of this 'Problem Play' a uniquely complete act of tragic imagination. For the rest, it seems to me that the machinery introduced to make for a happy ending does not work. The blunders, lies and contrivances of the disguised Duke lead to a final scene in which Mercy as well as Justice (the condemnation of Lucio) have their say before everybody is paired off in the best comic tradition: Claudio with Julietta, Angelo with Mariana, Lucio with a whore, and the Duke with a completely silent Isabella. A disappointment; but the first half is among the supreme achievements of the poet. The range and power of the verse would have captured any audience, gentle or simple; the principal characters are of the upper class, but their predicaments are of a kind understandable by all; and the striking contemporaneity of the issues at stake would have made the audience think hard about the prevalence of vice and the sometimes random interventions of Authority in the very streets they had traversed on the way to the theatre.

Othello represents a return to tragedy, with a plot as simple as that of *Measure for Measure* is compound. Here Shakespeare repeats something he had done in *Romeo and Juliet* and would do again in *The Winter's Tale*, playing his variations on an existing novella or poem; he seems to have been ready to turn his attention to almost any narrative, altering it under the powerful drive of his own interests and talents. After the Restoration the critic Thomas Rymer thought *Othello* silly or pointless, a fuss about the baiting of a black man, a 'bloody farce without salt or savour', with nonsense about a handkerchief, of which the moral seemed to be that 'maidens of quality' should not, 'without their parents' consent ... run away with blackamoors', and that 'all good wives [should] look well to their linen'. Rymer wrote in 1693, when different and restrictive notions about what was correct in tragedy had taken hold, and when attitudes toward black people were cruder. The slave trade was by then well established, and so was the rule that tragic heroes must be great men much concerned with honour; by Rymer's day the very idea of a black man might suggest a slave. Matters were not so clear-cut in Shakespeare's time, though one recalls that Aaron in *Titus Andronicus* refers quite proudly to his baby as a 'thick-lipp'd slave' (IV.ii.175).

Yet nobody in the play, not even his enemy Iago, expresses keen resentment that General Othello is black. Iago's principal grouse is that Othello preferred Cassio as his lieutenant, and Brabantio thinks his daughter's elopement is the result of a foreigner's witchcraft. On the other hand, the language of Roderigo and Iago in the opening scene outside Brabantio's house is certainly racist. But they are, after all, men of the gutter, and, as they speak, in the gutter. To the Duke and to Cassio and Desdemona and the other aristocratic characters (though not, of course, to Othello himself) his colour is an irrelevance.

There has been much dispute about Othello's origins, and the term 'Moor' is hard to define. Shakespeare uses it quite often – thirteen times of Aaron, more of Othello, mostly when Iago is speaking; but Desdemona uses it affectionately. As E. A. Honigmann points out in his Arden edition, the term was applied 'loosely to non-European races, little darker than many Europeans'. Londoners had first-hand experience of Moors, for an embassy from Barbary, on the coast of North Africa, remained in London for six months from August 1600. These visitors to the Elizabethan court were Mediterranean Muslims, and Shakespeare might well have encountered them. A contemporary historian of Africa describes them as honest and 'destitute of fraud and guile … very proud and high-minded, and wonderfully addicted unto wrath', as well as jealous and credulous. A portrait (1600–1) of the Moorish ambassador shows him to have the olive colouring of northern Africa. He looks more a master than a slave – Othello in his more magnificent moments.

One of the splendours of *Othello* is the inventiveness of its dialects – that is, the modes of speech appropriate to individual characters. Othello is orotund, talking as no Venetian does, with huge unabashed metaphors in stately succession. Iago is subtle and dangerous, projecting the deep obscenity of his mind on to his immediate society – more evil because of the foulness of his imagination, his total alienation, than Edmund in *King Lear*, more hateful than Thersites in *Troilus and Cressida*, for Thersites hates himself more than he hates humanity, and more dangerous than Apemantus in *Timon of Athens* because he uses misanthropy as a weapon, not just as the expression of a generalized loathing of human life. Iago has a place, lower than he feels he deserves, in a civilized society; the others are outsiders. Among the varieties of pain this tragedy can inflict on its audience is the pain of being forced to think of Iago as representing what must be understood as an inescapable part of any idea of society, just as Roderigo is an image of inevitable youthful folly. Cassio's slightly overdrawn, faintly libertine courtesy to women shows another aspect of this society, in a time of manners a little too highly wrought, gallantries so close to being seductive that Iago's slander of him has some space to work in.

Elizabethan curiosity about Venice arose partly because it was an example of what should, in the usual view, have been a faulty form of government, the republican; yet under this handicap (if one saw it as such) Venice had made itself rich and powerful and been the defender of Christian Europe against the Turk. It had long since achieved a mercantile magnificence of which the English, for all their growing enterprise and their new ostentation, were still far short. Venice was also admired on ecclesiastical grounds as the stubborn opponent of the Pope. At a popular level Venice had glamour. Like Italy more generally, it was associated with splendid courtesans, subtle poisons, and all the thrill of the vendetta – an aspect often on display in the London theatres, as we know from the works of Webster, Tourneur and Middleton. Less bloodthirsty than these contemporaries, Shakespeare set two of his plays in Venice, one of them having a strong interest in commercial venturing and usury, the other in military achievement – the defence of Cyprus (historically a failure) and the military presence, in a highly developed modern society, of many 'extravagant and wheeling strangers' (I.i.136).

Of course there is nothing specifically Venetian about jealousy. If we are to believe Freud, it is an emotion everybody has experienced, though reactions to it are normally less catastrophic than Othello's nightmare descent into the disgusting dungeon of Iago's fantasies. Jealousy interested Shakespeare; another, even more destructive variety is treated in *The Winter's Tale* and another, less convincingly, in *Cymbeline*. Since the emotion is featured also in *Hamlet*, one might venture to say that it engaged Shakespeare at some profound level of consciousness. Yet the infidelity of the Dark Lady of the Sonnets seems to be met with a sort of dismayed resignation rather than violent reaction, unlike these dramatic instances. Nevertheless it was possible to enact jealousy on the

Elizabethan stage without such extremes; see, for instance, Thomas Heywood's surprisingly delicate domestic tragedy *A Woman Killed with Kindness*, almost contemporary with *Othello*, but not a Globe play. The audiences of 1603 could respond to all types of jealousy, even when great personages were involved. The wrongs of the bold but virtuous Desdemona, the agonies of Othello at the hands of a tormentor expert in the pathological fantasies of jealousy, merely represented on a grand scale emotions which Elizabethan audiences, and their successors, could identify as their own.

Like *Hamlet*, *King Lear* reworks an anonymous old play, *The True Chronicle History of King Leir*, written about 1588 but not published till 1605. Shakespeare's play was entered in the Stationers' Register in 1607 as 'a book called Master William Shakespeare his history of King Lear as it was played before the King's Majesty upon St. Stephen's night at Christmas last, by his Majesty's servants playing usually at the Globe on the Bankside' – an unusually full entry intended to make it clear that this was not a revised version of the old play, recently published, but a new treatment of the subject. Since the differences between the two plays are so vast, the claim would not be hard to establish. These differences also demonstrate the speed at which the drama was changing. It is as if there were a kind of collusion between author and audience – a search for, and an acceptance of, greater refinement. *Lear* offers a much less straightforward return on the investment of audiences who had earlier come to the theatre with the expectation that they would see some simple sort of justice done on the stage: the great man falls but somehow good prevails, or anyway the survivors rally to sustain 'the gor'd state' (V.iii.321).

This is roughly true of the old *Leir*. Ancient Britain was in fashion, now that James ruled in England as well as Scotland; there was a new interest in a consolidated realm called Britain. Perhaps this was part of the reason why the old *Leir* was resuscitated in 1605. *Cymbeline* is another example, drawing as it does on the half-legendary ancient history of the kingdom of Britain. The stories of the two Lear/Leir plays are basically the same, but there are many differences of detail and emphasis. The thunder and lightning corresponding to Shakespeare's storm are meant, in the old play, to represent a heavenly intervention that saves the king from a murderer. In that play the king is restored to his throne and Cordelia survives.

G. K. Hunter remarks that it might be best to think of *King Leir* as a romance, with many similarities to other romance-adventure plays of its period. It treats of malice and exile, but 'it also shows…an unshakeable trust in God's providence and belief in the power of passive goodness to disarm active evil'. Wickedness, it is implied, cannot totally destroy the world of order and virtue. When the tragic action is over, the state remains to be run, and there are virtuous men to do the job.

Such is the consolatory pattern of *Macbeth*; and when Othello dies, there are those on stage who are already doing his office. It is harder to make the same claim for *King Lear*. The strongly Christian ethos of the old play has quite gone. Appeals to divine justice now turn out to be useless and ironical; indeed, all forms of justice, and Providence itself, are thwarted with a deliberation that shocked Dr Johnson. Why must Cordelia be murdered? No existing version of the story except Shakespeare's records this loss; coming as it does after sufferings that seem to be approaching their end, it is an extraordinary cruelty. The death of Cordelia, the torture of Gloucester, the agony of the old man on the heath tearing off his clothes in the storm, are, in Johnson's expression, 'contrary to the natural idea of justice', and the murder of Cordelia is, to Johnson, perhaps the worst instance, for it gratuitously violates 'the faith of the chronicles'. It was as if Shakespeare added it in order to be, within his profession, as cruel as Cornwall is in his play.

It has often been argued, and as often contested, that there was a darkness in the national mood in these early Jacobean years. The argument can certainly be made to seem plausible. For example, a sense that the health and stability of the world at large were in rapid decline was widespread. This was a subject of interest to John Donne, who wrote powerfully about it in his *Anniversaries*, including among the evidence of decay some of the discoveries of the new astronomy of Copernicus and Galileo: telescopes could show that the moon was not a perfect sphere, comets show that the heavens themselves, supposed to be pure, were corruptible; novae appeared in the sky when in principle such changes were impossible; venerable notions of the relation of sun to earth were called into question. ''Tis all in pieces, all coherence gone,' wrote Donne. There was learned opposition to such conclusions, but they were common enough, and old superstitious fears persisted. Gloucester in *King Lear* is sure that the scientific explanation of 'these late eclipses of the sun and moon' (I.ii.103) cannot dispel the belief that they are evil portents. (There had been solar and lunar eclipses in 1605.) 'Though the wisdom of nature can reason thus and thus, yet nature finds itself scourg'd by the sequent effects. Love cools, friendships fall off, brothers divide: in cities, mutinies, in countries, discord, in palaces, treason: and the bond crack'd between son and father... We have seen the best of our time' (I.ii.104–12).

The play also remembers the imagined link between these phenomena and the Terrors that, according to prediction, would precede the Last Days. *Lear* is a play conscious of apocalypse. It was a subject familiar to all, and probably dreaded by most, whether from study of the wall paintings in churches, where Doomsday was often represented over the chancel arch, or from the text of the Book of Revelation, now for the best part of a century accessible in the vernacular, and always, to this day, a source of anxiety as well as a manual of eschatological chronology. The idea of apocalypse seems to become urgent or concentrated at particular moments in history – at the ends of millennia or centuries, or on other dates found to be significant by students of the arithmetic of Revelation. At the turn of the twentieth century, apocalyptic prophecy of the biblical kind, usually predicting the Terrors that must come before the End, has been primarily associated with fundamentalist Christians, but it has been around for centuries in various other formulations by different schools of propagandists. An inscription in a seventh-century crypt near Poitiers in France reads: 'Alpha and Omega. The Beginning and the End. For all things become every day worse and worse, for the end is drawing near.'

The end of *King Lear* makes itself a figure for the end of the world: 'Is this the promis'd end?' asks Kent when the mad king enters with his dead daughter in his arms. 'Or image of that horror?' asks Edgar (V.iii.265–6). This is the play that best reflects the apocalyptic mood and the fear of the world's decay or decline; and the lines that best convey a real despair at the condition of humanity are those in which the virtuous Kent describes the base Oswald, a steward and go-between, a man to whom self-advancement at any cost in baseness is the motive of life:

> Such smiling rogues as these
> Like rats, oft bite the holy cords a-twain
> Which are t'intrinse t'unloose
>
> (II.ii.73–5)

The rats bite through the knots that bind families, friends and societies; the knots are sacred and cannot be untied, but are severed by the teeth of the vermin. It is a figure not only for Oswald but for Goneril and Regan and for Edmund, Gloucester's bastard son. To the virtuous, the symptoms of decay and moral collapse signify that the end must be nigh, but the rats have their own philosophies, purely naturalist in the bad sense, and are indifferent to the prospect of judgement. Such men assume that man is a wolf to man, that the breaking of social bonds only brings one nearer to nature, claiming that it is indeed conduct like Oswald's that is truly natural, not the patience and kindness of Kent and Cordelia.

King Lear makes many allusions to the Book of Job, Job being the archetype of patient suffering and also an image of the Terrors, an image of that horror; but after his testing, the biblical Job is finally restored to health and prosperity, whereas at the end of *Lear* Edgar (or Albany, who speaks the lines in the other version of the text) has no hope of a future happiness:

> The weight of this sad time we must obey,
> Speak what we feel, not what we ought to say:
> The oldest hath borne most; we that are young
> Shall never see so much, nor live so long.
>
> (V.iii.324–7)

It is a curiously flat way to end, but it does convey the idea that he sees no point in making up consoling obituaries or suggesting that all this suffering has a redemptive purpose. Edgar has already given us a message, if that is what we want, and it is far from consoling. In his meditation at the beginning of IV.i the fugitive reflects that having fallen so low he need fear no further fall. It is at this moment that he is suddenly confronted by his blinded father:

> O gods! Who is't can say 'I am at the worst'?
> I am worse than e'er I was...
> And worse I may be yet: the worst is not,
> So long as we can say, 'This is the worst.'

> (IV.i.25–8)

Keats, in his sonnet 'On Sitting Down to Read *King Lear* Once Again', describes the play as presenting 'the fierce dispute / Betwixt damnation and impassion'd clay', and that takes in a great part of its theme. What else lingers in the memory? Protraction: there is no end to the suffering, it is like the work of an ingenious torturer. Even when it seems that a tolerable conclusion is in sight, something happens to ensure that Cordelia and her father will not live together in mutual consolation but die wretched, she at the hands of a cheaply hired assassin. The dying Edmund says he would like to do some good before he goes, but he leaves it too late, and so his one generous impulse is frustrated. We cannot help thinking that it need not have been so, yet cannot escape the truth that it quite commonly is. The play offers neither its good characters nor its audience any relief from its cruelty. We remember that all those images of the Last Judgement, so abundant in Italian churches, are also full of cruel images of the damnation of impassioned clay.

The audiences of the day seemed to enjoy double-plotted

plays. In some of them – a prime example is Middleton's great tragedy *The Changeling* – the two plots are only loosely associated. But despite many flaws and slips in Shakespeare's plotting, the two plots of *King Lear* co-operate to extraordinary effect, and merge in the encounter between the mad Lear and the blind Gloucester (IV.vi), the most terrible moment in Shakespeare and perhaps in the whole of English drama. These are the moments that burn themselves into the mind: Lear arraigning his daughters in the imaginary trial during the storm; Gloucester set down by a tree to await the outcome of the battle, sitting blind and silent until the news of defeat means he must move on. He says he will not: Edgar counsels him, briskly and wisely: 'Men must endure / Their going hence even as their coming hither. / Ripeness is all. Come on.' 'And that's true too,' says the old man, who has heard that kind of wisdom before and now only wants to die (V.ii.9–11). Or perhaps, if we choose one image, we should think of Gloucester's enactment of suicide, his fall from an imaginary Dover cliff. Edgar makes one see the cliff, makes the old man think he has fallen off it, when all he has done is to make a jumping movement. It is the case of an actor enacting the pathos of the imaginary, as if to condemn the audience for being as much deceived as Gloucester himself.

It happened that in 1611 a performance of *Macbeth* at the Globe was witnessed by the astrologer-physician Simon Forman, who recorded the occasion in his 'book of plays'. Forman was a curious, rather louche character, and his career is of considerable interest to students of London life at the time. He had been imprisoned for practising medicine without a licence, but acquired one from Cambridge University in

1603. Among those who are known to have consulted him was Mary Mountjoy, with whose family Shakespeare had lodgings in 1604; her concern was a pregnancy that turned out to be false.

A better-known patient, who has of late become quite famous, was Emilia Lanier, née Bassano, the illegitimate daughter of a court musician, who had been the mistress of Henry Carey, the Lord Chamberlain, by repute a bastard of Henry VIII, and Shakespeare's sponsor at court until his death in 1596. Made pregnant by Carey, Bassano was married off to another musician, Alphonse Lanier. When she went to see Forman about a horoscope he seduced her, noting in his diary, where he duly recorded his amorous successes, that she was a woman who 'for lucre's sake will be a good fellow, for necessity doth compel'. Lanier was A. L. Rowse's choice for the role of the Dark Lady in the Sonnets; but a word in the manuscript that Rowse read as 'brown' turns out to be 'brave' and has nothing to do with her colouring; nor, for that matter, does the word 'dark' have exactly its modern connotations. Emilia, unlike the woman in Sonnet 127 and others, seems not to have been 'dark' in any sense, though as a member of a musical family she did play the virginals (Sonnet 128). In fact, her claim to the honour of being the Dark Lady is no greater than those of other contenders, who include the prostitute Lucy Negro and Mary Fitton, a maid of honour to Elizabeth and the mistress of William Herbert. A nephew of Sidney, Herbert was third earl of Pembroke – a great lord, patron of poets, and, with his brother Philip, the dedicatee of the Shakespeare First Folio in 1623. That Herbert was the Fair Youth of the Sonnets is an opinion that still has adherents; his chief rival is Henry Wriothesley, the Earl of Southampton, the dedicatee of *Venus and Adonis* and *The Rape of Lucrece.* That Fitton was the Dark Lady few now believe.

The reason for this excursus on Forman, his patients, and their lovers is that despite their dubious relevance to Shakespeare they do suggest something of the social and moral climate in which he lived, and of a demi-monde where quack doctors could, at any rate momentarily, belong to the same milieu as playwrights and great court officials – a milieu in which the social distance between actors and noblemen, astrologers and maids of honour, might be shortened when amorous or other interests supervened. As to Forman, he correctly forecast the date of his own death – not a difficult trick if you don't mind committing suicide. Emilia Lanier became a religious poet and is valued as a proto-feminist author. She had a long life, often a struggle, and died in her seventies in 1645. The revival of interest in her work, which includes 'Eve's Apology in Defence of Women', is a product of modern feminist scholarship. It was right to bring her back into literary history, for she was a learned and skilful poet.

Of all the major tragedies, *Macbeth* is the one most obviously in touch with current events. Written about 1606, it contains allusions to the Gunpowder Plot of 1605, a Catholic conspiracy to blow up Parliament and the King, and to the interrogation of conspirators. Back in 1559 Elizabeth had ordained that 'common interludes' (i.e. plays) should keep away from matters of religion and governance, and this injunction was repeated and occasionally enforced. In 1604, a play called *The Tragedy of Gowrie,* reflecting the new interest in Scottish history, was suppressed and is lost; it presumably dealt with the attempt of Lord Gowrie on the life of James VI of Scotland in 1600. In 1605, as we have seen before, Ben Jonson and his collaborators, working for a boys' company, were in trouble for writing *Eastward Ho!*, a play in which they satirized James's English court and the incursion of many unwelcome Scotsmen into England. It was not very likely that Shakespeare's Scottish play, performed by the company the King himself sponsored, would offer anything subversive, and in many respects *Macbeth* is a tribute to the King and his lineage, supposedly stretching back to Banquo and forward via his descendants 'to th' crack of doom' (IV.i.117). It is, under one aspect, a celebration of the new dynasty. Using the relevant history as chronicled in Holinshed, his favourite historical source, Shakespeare did not hesitate to blacken the character of the historical Macbeth and to make Duncan a virtuous, even saintly figure, which he was not.

Perhaps the most interesting topical connection of *Macbeth* with the Gunpowder Plot is its repeated use of the words 'equivocation', 'equivocator', and 'equivocates', and more generally the equivocation of the play itself. The words are not often found elsewhere in the canon. In a contemporary sense, 'equivocation' meant the moral licence given to priests under torture to avoid giving straight answers to their interrogators – a specialized application of the more general sense of 'using (the word) in more than one sense, ambiguity or uncertainty of meaning...' (*OED*, which gives a 1599 example of its application to Jesuits). The importance of the witches or Weird Sisters suggests an appeal to the King's well-known interest in witchcraft, and they make equivocal prophecies (a tradition of ambiguity or equivocation in prophecy stretched back to the Delphic Oracle). Shakespeare gives them a quasi-philosophical scope; what the future makes of the present situation is equivocal; time is the agent of equivocation. The decision to murder Duncan, which for a moment might go either way, occurs at a pause in time, a kind of interim between thought or intention and act during which past, present and future are equivocally held together; fair cannot be separated from foul, lost from won, the future from the instant. These memorable lines of Brutus's in *Julius Caesar* also describe such a moment:

> Between the acting of a dreadful thing
> And the first motion, all the interim is
> Like a phantasma or a hideous dream.

> (II.i.63–5)

There is no space here to develop the theme by examining lexical minutiae; the point is that a word like 'equivocation' opens up a semantic area in which time past, present and future must be dealt with. The word will affect what the Porter says as much as it affects the prophecies of the Weird Sisters, and it controls the language as well as the actions of Macbeth. The art of soliloquy, much developed in *Hamlet*, now acquires new force as the means by which a man trapped in that temporal interim can convey the almost frantic exercise of equivocating conscience and intellect. 'This supernatural soliciting / Cannot be ill, cannot be good,' reasons Macbeth (I.iii.130–1); and in his most celebrated soliloquy:

> If it were done, when 'tis done, then 'twere well
> It were done quickly. If th' assassination
> Could trammel up the consequence, and catch
> With his surcease, success; that but this blow
> Might be the be-all and the end-all – here,
> But here, upon this bank and shoal of time,
> We'ld jump the life to come.

> (I.vii.1–7)

There is little of comparable intensity in all of Shakespeare.

Granted that the chronology is uncertain, *Antony and Cleopatra* was close in time to *King Lear, Macbeth,* and *Timon of Athens. Coriolanus* was not much later, so we have an unparalleled output of masterpieces in the space of perhaps three years, and an astonishing variety of topics and settings. Looking at the list, one again feels some wonder at the talents of the boys who played Goneril, Lady Macbeth, Volumnia and Cleopatra. It is now thought that they continued, presumably in a sort of falsetto, until the age of eighteen or twenty; and anybody lucky enough to have seen Mark Rylance as Cleopatra in the modern Bankside Globe will know that a mature man can play Cleopatra with splendid effect. Still, it remains an extraordinary feat. Shakespeare makes a sort of in-joke about it when he has his Cleopatra say she will kill herself rather than be taken to Rome and forced to see 'some squeaking Cleopatra boy my greatness' (V.ii.220). He could hardly have risked that line if his own Cleopatra squeaked or merely 'boyed' the queen.

This play deals with another cardinal moment of history, the victory of Octavius, later Augustus, at the battle of Actium. This battle cleared the way for an empire based on Rome, not Alexandria; so it was thought decisive for the West, especially for Christian states, such as Britain, that had been part of the Roman Empire. Elizabeth's propagandists claimed that she inherited an imperial charisma from Constantine, the first Christian emperor, said to have been born of an English mother (St Helena), who later discovered the True Cross and the Holy Sepulchre at Jerusalem. When Octavius, close to victory, says 'the time of universal peace is near, / Prove this a prosp'rous day, the three-nook'd world / Shall bear the olive freely' (IV.vi.4–6) he is referring to the so-called Augustan Peace, the years when Providence ensured that Christ would be born into a world at least momentarily at rest from conflict. (The 'nooks' into which he divides the world are Europe, Asia and Africa.) A reminder of the Augustan Peace would not come amiss in a play written in the reign of James I, who aspired to be a great peacemaker and was later celebrated as such by Rubens in the magnificent ceiling paintings in the Banqueting House in Whitehall.

However, the true focus of the play, for which Shakespeare again drew on Plutarch, lies in the contrast between melting Egypt (the idea derives from the annual flooding of the Nile, but also suggests the dissolute life of Cleopatra's court) and rigid, stony Rome: between rigid Octavius and melting Antony. Those opening lines criticize Antony for his shameful enslavement to Cleopatra (as his patron god Hercules succumbed to Omphale and was compelled to sit at a spinning-wheel). His rejection of the messenger from Rome finds him already thinking in terms of hardness and softness: 'Let Rome in Tiber melt, and the wide arch / Of the rang'd empire fall' (I.i.33–4). But Rome will not melt like Egypt.

Antony and Cleopatra was once thought too difficult to stage because of its profusion of very brief scenes; but it came to be understood that there need be no break between them, and that having a Roman scene on one side of the stage did not preclude having an Alexandrian scene on the other side. The rapid to and fro between parts of the empire is an important part of the story, and the play, now admired for its combination of political altercation and high poetry, is often performed. The scope is imperial; a quarrel between its two principal figures would be 'As if the world should cleave' (III.iv.31), and

Antony at Actium loses 'half the bulk o' th' world' (III.xi.64). To Cleopatra he is 'Lord of lords' (IV.viii.16) and 'the crown o' th' earth' (IV.xv.63). In her posthumous eulogy he exists on the level of myth:

> His legs bestrid the ocean, his rear'd arm
> Crested the world, his voice was propertied
> As all the tuned spheres, and that to friends;
> But when he meant to quail and shake the orb,
> He was as rattling thunder.
>
> (V.ii.82–6)

If Antony is compared to Hercules, Cleopatra melts into Isis/Aphrodite. In the beautiful little scene (IV.iii) when the soldiers interpret the strange music (in the air? under the earth?) as presaging the departure of 'the god Hercules, whom Antony lov'd' (16), Shakespeare deliberately says 'Hercules' and not 'Bacchus', the god of carousing, though 'Bacchus' is what Plutarch wrote. At that point in the play we do not need reminding of Antony's 'lascivious wassails', as Octavius calls his dissipations (I.iv.56), but of the hero, the demigod, in defeat.

When appropriate there is exuberant celebration of love and luxury, with great set pieces like Enobarbus's description of Cleopatra and her barge on the river Cydnus:

> The barge she sat in, like a burnish'd throne,
> Burnt on the water. The poop was beaten gold,
> Purple the sails, and so perfumed that
> The winds were love-sick with them; the oars were silver,
> Which to the tune of flutes kept stroke, and made
> The water which they beat to follow faster,
> As amorous of their strokes...
>
> (II.ii.191–7)

The wonder is that this passage stays very close to the passage in the Plutarch translation from which it is drawn: 'the poop…was of gold, the sails of purple, and the oars of silver, which kept stroke in rowing after the sound of the music of flutes, oboes, citherns, viols…'

The glamour of such passages, and the magnificence of the closing scenes, should not allow us to forget that the play has strong political interests. The verse in the scenes of political dealing is equally powerful. Here, as a single example, is Octavius meditating the response of the common people to the reputations of great men (in this case, the younger Pompey):

> It hath been taught us from the primal state
> That he which is was wish'd, until he were;
> And the ebb'd man, ne'er lov'd till ne'er worth love,
> Comes dear'd by being lack'd. This common body,
> Like to a vagabond flag upon the stream,
> Goes to and back, lackeying the varying tide,
> To rot itself with motion.

> (I.iv.41–7)

(Flags are water weeds.) A Jacobean audience, which would revel in the richness of the more lyrical parts of the play, could also, one supposes, deal with meditations as knotted as this – with the language of a cold politician who comes closest to melting only at the end, when he views the dead body of Cleopatra and speaks lines which are among the most admired in Shakespeare:

> she looks like sleep,
> As she would catch another Antony
> In her strong toil of grace.

> (V.ii.346–8)

As in Horace's great ode on the victory at Actium, the last lines are reserved for a reluctant tribute to a hated but beautiful enemy.

Of *Timon of Athens* I shall say little. As we have it in the Folio it is clearly an unfinished play, and not every word of it is by Shakespeare. The nature of its interest seems to be twofold. First, it is an unusually schematic play – one can see the skeleton, and some parts are elaborately filled in while others appear not to have got beyond sketches. Secondly, having shown Timon's collapse into total misanthropy, there is no relief from the necessity to express without remission a hatred of humanity. Shakespeare probably came across the story of Timon in Plutarch's *Life of Antony*, where it occurs in a sort of excursus. He may also have known a dialogue by the second-century Greek satirist Lucian, which also deals with Timon's foolish prodigality and later misanthropy; like Shakespeare's hero, Lucian's Timon digs for roots and finds gold.

The opening scenes of the play schematically illustrate Timon's intemperance. First he is the overgenerous man who dissipates his great wealth on lavish presents and dinners for flatterers. Curiously, Shakespeare constructed an elaborate dialogue between a poet and a painter who are sycophantically competing for the honour of best portraying the great benefactor. This highly finished scene is a version of the contest known as the *paragone*, a match or competition, in Italy a formalized dialogue argument between rival artists, perhaps a painter and a sculptor, or, as here, a painter and a poet, about the merits of their ways of depicting the moral qualities of a patron. The participants are just as venal as the other tradesmen who enter shortly afterwards. Unlike much that comes later, in the middle of the play, the dialogue of this *paragone* is written in Shakespeare's most difficult later manner, with much fleetingly metaphoric language that would be hard to follow in the theatre, even by audiences much better at listening than we are. But it seems possible that the play was never put on. The polished scenes are overelaborate and show the marks of prefabrication. This is true not only of the *paragone* but of the set piece on the Banquet of Sense in I.ii.122ff., structurally balanced by its counterpart in the tasteless banquet of III.vi.65ff. Other scenes are in an undeveloped state, metrically defective and sketchy. Timon's desertion by his friends, one after another, is awkward and perfunctory. The procession of visitors to the hermit Timon is also clumsily contrived.

Yet the play must have been started ambitiously, a study in temperamental extremes and the corruption of art and manners by greed. As a study of a man who cannot properly live either in society or out of it, *Timon* has moments of alarming power, notably in the hate speech of the exiled millionaire and the repulsive Apemantus. Yet their diatribes against whoredom and greed, against nature itself, lack the depth of the passages in *King Lear* which they inevitably recall. The hero's tragic absurdity arises not from the general human condition but from his excesses, whether in the role of universal giver or archetypal misanthrope. 'The middle of humanity thou never knewest,' as Apemantus tells him, 'but the extremity of both ends' (IV.iii.300–1). The madness of this position is made plain enough by Timon's argument that the motive force of the universe is thievery:

> The sun's a thief, and with his great attraction
> Robs the vast sea; the moon's an arrant thief,

And her pale fire she snatches from the sun;
The sea's a thief, whose liquid surge resolves
The moon into salt tears; the earth's a thief,
That feeds and breeds by a composture stol'n
From gen'ral excrement, each thing's a thief.
The laws, your curb and whip, in their rough power
Has uncheck'd theft.

(IV.iii.436–4)

(The last phrase means 'has unlimited power to thieve'.) Somewhere behind this powerful rant there may be a memory of an opposite thesis, which argues that the motive power of the universe is love – what Dante called the love that moves the sun and the other stars. But *Timon of Athens*, if one sets aside the hapless benevolence of Timon's steward Flavius, is a bitter, loveless exercise.

Coriolanus is the last of the tragedies and the last great achievement of English drama in that genre. Once again the source is in Plutarch's *Lives*, but now the scene is a much earlier Rome, after the expulsion of the kings a republic troubled by conflicting political interests. In one sense the politics of the play is abstract – it examines the relation between disparate social orders, between the people and their leaders, the rich and the poor, the military ruler and the mob faced by a foreign enemy. The external threat requires the patrician class to breed heroes and generals who believe that honours won in battle are the highest rewards – the more wounds sustained, the nobler the sufferer and the more entitled to recognition by the state. The working class is more interested in getting enough to eat than in fighting, and is therefore scorned by the warrior caste, of whom Coriolanus is the prime exemplar. Much to his disgust, the people have acquired two crafty tribunes to represent them. Their managerial skills work on Coriolanus's ungovernable temper to have him exiled.

Less abstractly, contemporaries might well have seen the play as concretely relevant to the political situation of their own day, the early years of James's reign. James, as we have seen, disliked crowds, and in 1607 (the probable date of the play) he issued a proclamation deploring the fact that 'the meanest sort of people have presumed lately to assemble themselves riotously in multitudes'. That is what the common people are doing at the start of *Coriolanus* – riotously assembling, and 'rubbing the poor itch of their opinion', as Coriolanus puts it in his appallingly provocative opening speech (I.i.65–6). As we saw in discussing *Troilus and Cressida*, opinion is a poor thing anyway; even if it happens to be right, it is a lesser thing than truth.

Popular disturbances in the Midlands were at this time a matter of some concern; they were often associated with dearth, or with wages depressed by inflation, or unemployment caused by enclosures. Once the land was turned to pasture, many agricultural labourers became redundant and very likely disaffected; 'sturdy beggars' were a familiar and perhaps a growing problem. Shakespeare was decidedly unsentimental about mobs, but usually allows individual members of a crowd to show some wit. Crowds can be at once good-humoured, funny, and dangerous, as they are shown to be in the Jack Cade scenes of *2 Henry VI* and in *Julius Caesar*. Shakespeare might well have seen a Midlands crowd in his youth, and again in late life when he was himself involved in troubles arising from an attempt to enclose some open fields in the Stratford area;

Shakespeare, as it happens, opposed the attempt, not because it would be an added affliction to the poor, but because he had an investment in tithes that would be affected by the move. But that complicated tale belongs to the poet's last years.

A Globe audience, accustomed to a certain stereotyping according to class, might well have seen in the proletariat of *Coriolanus* a certain distorted image of themselves. And there were other parallels to consider. The resemblance between Coriolanus and Essex was pointed out at the time – both were soldiers, fierce aristocrats, and favourites; but it was Essex's reputation as an 'ungoverned governor', a rash and arrogant general, that made the comparison plausible. Essex stormed his way to the executioner's block; Coriolanus was driven into exile and the arms of the enemies of Rome.

It would, however, be wrong to treat *Coriolanus* as a close comment on Elizabethan/Jacobean politics in this narrow sense. It touches on topics so general and so intractable that they remain with us today – for example, the proper education of elites, the inequitable distribution of wealth, the relations of power within the community, the duty of submission to law and perhaps to custom, and the inevitability in government of machiavellian prevarication and even corruption, awareness of which cannot erase the citizen's duty of service, of patriotism.

Coriolanus is the harshest and coldest of the great tragedies; like its hero it is lonely and terrible – 'Like to a lonely dragon, that his fen / Makes fear'd and talk'd of more than seen' (IV.i.30–1). Shakespeare invented the little scene of the Roman ladies and the boy Martius (I.iii) to tell us obliquely about the defects of Coriolanus's education. Such a mother, exulting in blood and wounds, applauding the little boy's mauling of a butterfly ('one on's father's moods' [I.iii.66]), is unlikely to bring up a child fit for rule in a complex society. He and his friends are enemies of the people, full of contempt and anger but much less clever than the tribunes, whom Shakespeare makes baser than they are in Plutarch. Plutarch, unlike Shakespeare, was a republican.

The play literalizes the notion of the body politic. It opens with a display of plebeian resentment of Coriolanus, to be followed at once by Menenius's exposition of the necessary interdependence of the parts of the body, with the upper classes as the necessary belly, source of strength and nourishment to the other parts. Thereafter allusions to body parts abound, sometimes as jokes – 'the great toe of this assembly' (I.i.155) – and sometimes very serious. The plebs have votes – in Elizabethan parliamentary terminology, 'voices' – and these issue from the stinking mouths and tongues of a crowd who, following the custom, require to see the candidate's wounds in return for their suffrage. Coriolanus, despite urgent counselling from friends who have more patience with the demands of electioneering, shows himself unwilling to display his wounds so that the citizens could 'put tongues into those wounds and speak for them' (II.iii.6–7). Coriolanus needs the voices but wishes the owners would clean their teeth. So these voices, issuing from the dirty and diseased mouths of the people, found another purpose: they rejected Coriolanus, hooting him into exile as he made his defiant responses: 'I banish you!' (III.iii.123), and 'There is a world elsewhere' (III.iii.135). As to the bodies of the nobility, they bear their scars proudly; as Wilson Knight long ago pointed out, Coriolanus's body is represented as a battered war machine rather than a human being of flesh and blood.

Names, which define such persons, assume great importance. Coriolanus gets his from the city he stormed in a one-man assault. Such a name is, in Shakespeare's vocabulary, an 'addition', and not intrinsic to the body it is attached to – a sense familiar from *King Lear* I.i.136 and other texts. The use of this name leads directly to Coriolanus's death, when Aufidius challenges his use of it. Early in the play Coriolanus asks a favour of his general after the battle: that a poor prisoner from Corioli who had done him some service in the past should be spared from slavery. The request is granted, but Coriolanus has forgotten the name of his benefactor. In Plutarch the request is on behalf of 'an old friend of mine, an honest wealthy man'. This is a significant little change, for in Plutarch the name of the friend is not mentioned or needed, and Coriolanus therefore has no occasion to forget it. In Shakespeare the man is poor, and even his name – an 'addition' – is lost.

When Coriolanus in exile goes into the house of his enemy Aufidius, a remarkable bit of dialogue follows, in which 'name' has taken the place of 'voice':

AUF: Whence com'st thou? What would'st thou? Thy name?...
COR: If, Tullus,
  Not yet thou know'st me, and, seeing me, does not
  Think me for the man I am, necessity
  Commands me name myself.
AUF: What's thy name?
COR: A name unmusical to the Volscian ears,
  And harsh in sound to thine.
AUF: Say, what's thy name?
  Thou hast a grim appearance, and thy face
  Bears a command in't; though thy tackle's torn
  Thou show'st a noble vessel. What's thy name?
COR: Prepare thy brow to frown. Know'st thou me yet?

AUF: I know thee not. Thy name?

COR: My name is Caius Martius, who hath done

    To thee particularly, and all the Volsces,

    Great hurt and mischief; thereto witness may

    My surname, Coriolanus.

                        (IV.v.53–68)

This is a moment of protracted recognition virtually unique in Shakespeare, and matched only by the long recognition scene in *Pericles*, to be mentioned later, where the effect is quite different. The play on 'name' is echoed when near the end of the play Menenius, formerly a close friend, seeks to interview Coriolanus in the Volscian camp outside Rome, wishing to implore him to call off the assault. He is sure his name will get him past the guards. But they mock it, and the power he attributes to it, and send him away.

This trick of hammering away at a single word is one that Shakespeare used more and more. This insistence on the word 'name' repeats the effect of the reiteration of 'voice' in II.iii; both words are central to the dialect, as it were, of this gnarled and bitter play. Aufidius's final plot against the hero depends on his pride in his name and on the fact that in giving up the siege of Rome he yielded to no man but to a woman, his mother. So he could lose his great surname and be called by Aufidius a 'boy of tears' (V.vi.100). The last of the tragic heroes is, in the end, less than a complete man by his own standards, and for that and other reasons – his anger, his hatred of the people – might no more than Timon have had the sympathy of Jacobean audiences. And for whatever reason, *Coriolanus*, in some respects the most intense, the most demanding of the tragedies, was Shakespeare's last. How he changed after he gave up tragedy is matter for another chapter.

The Blackfriars monastic compound, no longer in use by the Dominican friars who originally owned it, was situated a good stone's throw from St Paul's on the north bank of the Thames, not quite opposite the theatres on the other bank, but offering an easy crossing to men concerned with both Globe and Blackfriars. Because of its ecclesiastical past it was a 'liberty', and so not under the jurisdiction of the City. It was a large cluster of buildings, some used for residential purposes, and a theatre had been built in the old refectory by 1576. The theatre was in use in the 1580s, when John Lyly among others put on plays with boy actors, but in 1584 it was closed.

James Burbage, the father of Richard the actor and himself an actor, had built the Theatre in nearby Shoreditch in 1576, and later took part in the construction of the Globe, an enterprise in which the Burbages had a major share of the profits. With businesslike foresight James Burbage now decided that he and the company needed an indoor theatre, so in 1596 he bought property in the Blackfriars with a view to setting up such a theatre within the precinct, this time for the use of his adult associates in Shakespeare's company, then the Lord Chamberlain's Men.

However, he was prevented from using it by the protest of the well-to-do residents of the precinct, who successfully petitioned the Privy Council to forbid the development. When

James Burbage died in 1597 his son Richard took over, leasing the playhouse to the Children of the Chapel, who were allowed to play and now, in circumstances mentioned earlier, gave the adult companies some strong competition. But they got into trouble on several occasions, terminally in 1608 when they performed Chapman's *Conspiracy of Charles Duke of Biron*. This tragedy gave such offence to the French that the company was suppressed. And so at last, in 1608, the Blackfriars theatre became available to Shakespeare's company, which began to play there in 1609. Shakespeare was one of seven lessors, paying one seventh of the annual rent of forty pounds.

Burbage's plan was thus realized long after his death by the company, now, of course, known as the King's Men. Their interest in this new venue was inspired largely by financial considerations, for although the new 'private' theatre was much smaller than the Globe, it was not open to the weather, and the lowest admission charge was six times as much as in the parent theatre. Evidently the company's playwrights would now work with this indoor theatre in mind, but without ignoring the needs of the Globe; Shakespeare's last plays were almost certainly performed at both theatres, thereby satisfying two audiences that were nevertheless inevitably acquiring different tastes and expectations.

Blackfriars performances continued, as it were out of habit, to be given in the afternoon, but the constitution of the audience was changing. The Globe could accommodate five times as many, but the higher prices at the Blackfriars more than eliminated the discrepancy, and in the end the new theatre made more money than the Globe for Shakespeare and his colleagues.

Private theatres grew more numerous in the years that

followed, until they and not the open-air arenas were the norm, and they obviously had more influence on later theatrical history. The residents of the precinct renewed their objections to the theatre, one of which was that the coaches of theatre patrons now blocked the streets. This time the petitioners tried their luck with the City authorities, and succeeded in getting an order to the effect they desired, prescribing a prison sentence for dilatory coachmen, but it was rarely if ever applied. Later protests also failed. In 1633 the Privy Council pointed out that the congestion could be reduced if patrons would arrive by water, as they easily might; but nothing followed, and the Blackfriars playhouse remained in use until Parliament closed all theatres in 1642. It was knocked down in 1655.

With a smaller stage and auditorium, the Blackfriars charged not only the sixpence for admission, which got one into a gallery, but an extra shilling for a seat on a bench in the pit. Gallants who hired a stool and sat on the stage itself paid more. There is much learned conjecture about the design of the stages, but the Blackfriars was not in essence so different from the Globe that transfer of plays from one to the other would have been a difficult business.

The most splendid indoor theatrical performances of the day were the aristocratic court masques, with their brilliant costumes, stage machinery, lighting, and music; and these qualities could be better imitated (though doubtless with considerable reductions of scale) at the Blackfriars than in the large open-air theatres. As to comfort, there was no comparison between the Globe on a cold damp afternoon and the shelter and comparative warmth of the indoor theatre, bright with candlelight and offering the subtler music of lutes rather than the drums and trumpets of the Globe. The rich, in their boxes or on the stage, were now closest to the action, which was not the case at the Globe but has been the case ever since, except at such unusual modern London venues as the Roundhouse and the new Globe.

The King's Men playwrights and actors were professionals who could adapt to new conditions. They must have enjoyed the facilities, though of course they had been long accustomed to indoor performances at court and elsewhere. Out of doors the only way to establish that the action was taking place in darkness was to say so, as in the opening lines of *Hamlet* or at the murder of Banquo in *Macbeth* III.iii. Indoors one imagines that acting would be less stentorian, more subtle, like the music.

The mass audience of the Globe did not survive the closing of the theatres in 1642, but the richer customers were soon provided for, often by William Davenant, who was working as a playwright as early as the 1620s and became a licensed theatre manager after the Restoration. Davenant thus represents a certain theatrical continuity. He rewrote some of Shakespeare's plays for the more civilized Restoration stage, and even claimed to be Shakespeare's illegitimate son. In these somewhat unexpected ways the Shakespeare family connection with the London theatre was sustained.

'Romance' is the generic title nowadays given to *Pericles*, *Cymbeline*, *The Winter's Tale* and *The Tempest*, with *The Two Noble Kinsmen* sometimes counted in. These plays do show a difference in manner from the Globe plays, and some of the change has been ascribed to the move to Blackfriars. Other factors have been adduced: a new interest in beautiful and virtuous girls, appropriate to the father of two nubile daughters; or a more general softening, a cultivated repose, possibly in the wake of some kind of breakdown, of which *Timon of Athens* might have been a symptom. But by far the least probable of these conjectures is the one that presupposes the romances to radiate calm acceptance. They contain verse almost as dense and complex, as harsh and troubled, as can be found in *Coriolanus* and *Timon.*

Cymbeline and *The Winter's Tale* can reasonably be called tragicomedies, although in so far as there were prescriptions for tragicomedy Shakespeare violated the one that says that in this genre characters are brought near to death but do not die; for Cloten dies in *Cymbeline* and Mamillius in *The Winter's Tale. Cymbeline* was included among the tragedies in the Folio of 1623. Nomenclature is a minor problem, but all these plays end happily enough after a lengthy series of dangerous adventures; and so they might as well be given their modern appellation, romances. One should nevertheless bear in mind that it is their plots and not their language that earn them this title.

In some important respects the model romance was *Pericles.* It is quite like the romance plays of an earlier epoch, some of which were being revived about this time (circa 1608). *Pericles* was not included in the Folio of 1623, perhaps because the editors of that volume, Shakespeare's friends Heminges and Condell, did not trust the provenance of the text; or possibly they thought that too much of the play was evidently by another hand than Shakespeare's, though that consideration did not lead them to exclude *Henry VIII.* There is a quarto edition (1609) of *Pericles,* but it is very corrupt. The play has the unusual distinction of having a novella based on it, and editors, who have a rough ride with this play, have to take the novella into account. The difference in quality between parts of the play is great enough to support the conjecture that Shakespeare reworked only parts of it. Nearly everybody agrees that apart from a few fine moments in the earlier acts, the voice of Shakespeare is fully audible only from the beginning of Act III.

The romance story was popular and ancient. Pericles loses his wife and his newborn daughter in a great storm at sea. After wandering about the world for years in deepening melancholia, he is reunited, first with his daughter, now a young woman, and then with his wife. Here are some lines from Pericles's farewell to his supposedly dead wife before she is thrown overboard:

> A terrible childbed hast thou had, my dear,
> No light, no fire. Th' unfriendly elements
> Forgot thee utterly, nor have I time
> To give thee hallow'd to thy grave, but straight
> Must cast thee, scarcely coffin'd, in the ooze,
> Where, for a monument upon thy bones
> The e'er remaining lamps, the belching whale
> And humming water must o'erwhelm thy corpse,
> Lying with simple shells.
>
> (III.i.56–64)

The mixture of figures here is characteristically demanding: that whales should be said to 'belch' is easily understood, but 'remaining', 'humming', and 'simple' are strange; the 'remaining lamps' follow the suggestion of a tomb or monument, which is perforce replaced by these watery phenomena, which do not commemorate but overwhelm. But belching and humming are bad accompaniments to a burial, and when the body comes to rest it lies with 'simple' shells – simple by contrast with the furious water above them, or with the body that has joined them. This is an early warning to those who find the last plays simple; not even the word 'simple' is simple.

Fine things are to be found not only in such passages of lamentation but even in the brothel scene (IV.vi), where Marina's indignation is more powerful than the persuasions of her captors and her customer; she is 'able to freeze the god Priapus' (IV.vi.3–4). And yet most memorable is Boult's defence against her virtuous anger when she condemns his trade: 'What would you have me do? Go to the wars, would you? Where a man may serve seven years for the loss of a leg, and have not money enough in the end to buy him a wooden one?' (IV.vi.170–3). We are reminded that virtue comes less easily to sturdy rogues and masterless men. Marina's advice – that he should give up brothel work and find a cleaner job as a garbageman or assistant hangman – shows a lack of sympathy proper to her caste.

However, the grandest moment of the play is the recognition scene between Pericles and Marina (V.i). The moment of total recognition is protracted to a point at which it might have been thought to verge on the ridiculous; Pericles has ample evidence of the girl's identity but goes on asking for more. And the effect is so far from ridiculous that it might deserve to be called sublime. Marina now is transfigured, magical, born of the sea in a tempest, so 'not of any shores' (103). The verse takes on a rapt, almost liturgical quality, to be paralleled, I think, nowhere else in the canon:

> Prithee, speak.
> Falseness cannot come from thee, for thou lookest

> Modest as Justice, and thou seem'st a palace
> For the crown'd Truth to dwell in.
>
> (V.i.119–22)

Pericles is so intensely moved that he has to ask Helicanus to strike him, put him 'to present pain' (191), to save him from dying of joy. Even so he requires more proof, more names, narratives, explanations before acknowledging complete recognition. Then, finally convinced that he has recovered his lost daughter, he blesses her, calls for fresh garments, and hears 'the music of the spheres' (229), that normally inaudible token of universal harmony. Happy endings usually involve feasting or marriage; almost none can compare with the solemn splendour of this one which, it might almost be said, deals with resurrection.

Yet one may think of this achievement as a deliberate professional experiment. Recognition had always been a reasonably straightforward element of dramatic technique; it is studied in Aristotle's *Poetics*. But at this stage in his career Shakespeare seems to have been obsessed by this vital dramaturgical moment, for he develops it in several different ways. In *Pericles* he makes it last so long that the auditor wants to call out to help him to the end. *Cymbeline* has so many brief and rapid recognitions (V.v) that readers differ in their tallies of how many there are. The device is there extended to the borders of farce, and one might for a moment wonder whether it is not meant to appeal to the taste and humour of the supposedly smarter audience at Blackfriars.

If so, this pile of recognitions was not the only respect in which this play was fashionable. Now that England and Scotland shared a king, and the term 'Britain' was being used to cover both kingdoms, the theatre was showing a new interest in ancient Britain. John Fletcher wrote a play (*Bonduca*) about Boadicea for the King's Men in 1611; the British courageously resist the Roman invaders yet learn from them the elements of civility and honour. That idea is also present in *Cymbeline*, which is an extraordinary mixture of genres. It is in part a history play – Cymbeline was thought to have reigned in Britain at the time of the birth of Christ – and the story concerns the valour of the ancient Britons in refusing tribute to the Romans (even the blockhead Cloten answers the Roman demands with noble defiance) until they chose to give it; they defend their heritage but are grateful to be introduced to Roman civilization. There is not much attempt at the historical perspective of which we know Shakespeare to have been capable; Iachimo is a wicked Renaissance Italian, not an ancient Roman, and Cymbeline's queen is a wicked woman from any epoch, or perhaps a witch from fairy tale.

The stories of the wager on Imogen's virtue and of the king's lost sons are typical romance themes and must be brought together to provide a suitable ending. While the process continues we hear some wonderfully gnarled and strange late-Shakespearian verse; sometimes the characters addressed do not understand what is being said, as in the scene between Cloten and his wicked mother (II.iii) and when Imogen fails to grasp the point of Iachimo's rodomontade when he is planning to seduce her.

Indeed, it is sometimes hard to avoid the feeling that the author is teasing the audience. The oddest of his jokes is the story of how Cloten dresses himself in the clothes of Posthumus to avenge an insult of Imogen's (Cloten, she says, is not worthy to wear Posthumus's 'mean'st garment' [II.iii.133–56], so he proposes to rape her while wearing her husband's clothes). From what we already know about Cloten we would expect the clothes to be an absurdly bad fit, but he declares that they fit very well (IV.i.2ff.), and when Imogen comes upon his headless body she mistakes it for her husband's: 'I know the shape of 's leg; this is his hand, / His foot Mercurial, his Martial thigh, / The brawns of Hercules...' (IV.ii.309–11). She recognizes the clothes but imagines she can identify this splendid body as well.

There are other tricks, including a repetitive interest in clothes (nowhere explained clearly, and although audiences may enjoy these mystifications, they are not what audiences mostly admire in this play: that is the character of Imogen – strong, courteous, eloquent, and courageous – a part much valued by good actresses). At the end Posthumus fails to recognize Imogen in boy's clothes and knocks her down, whereupon there follows a little dialogue that probably sounded as surprising and exquisite at the first performance as it still does; it was a favourite of Tennyson's, who died with the relevant page open before him:

> IMO: Why did you throw your wedded lady from you?
> Think you are upon a lock, and now
> Throw me again.
> POS: Hang there like fruit, my soul,
> Till the tree die!
>
> (V.v.261–4)

The Winter's Tale is a more serious play, but it continues the experiments in recognition. Once again parents are separated from one another and from their children, this time on a false accusation of adultery, to be reunited, after much woe, a generation later. A gap of sixteen years occurs between the opening scenes which enact the disastrous breach and the scenes in which recognitions and pardons will heal it. In this play Shakespeare simply inserts a speech by Time, announcing the lapse of these years; he will face a very similar problem in *The Tempest,* and solve it differently.

In the final scene of the play, Hermione, believed dead for all of those sixteen years, is restored to her husband. She is presented to him as a statue, suitably aged, and then she moves. To support the point that Shakespeare is experimenting with recognitions, one may note his solution of the problem (unsolved in *Pericles*) that he had to arrange two tremendously important recognitions by Leontes: of his daughter Perdita, and of his wife Hermione. Here Shakespeare avoids the risk of losing effectiveness through having two consecutive recognition scenes by making the meeting with Perdita a matter of report, even rather flippant report, by gentlemen who had witnessed it (V.ii). Thus he avoids having to do two scenes of great solemnity and reserves the major emotional impact for the moment when the statue of Hermione miraculously moves.

The story is based on a romance by Shakespeare's old enemy Robert Greene; but there is little of romance in the torrid opening scenes. When Leontes allows his mind to be obsessed with the thought of Hermione's adultery with his guest Polixenes, his language has an ugliness not encountered before in any play. Leontes's violent jealousy is quite different from Othello's, and a world away from the unconvincing reaction of Posthumus when falsely informed of Imogen's infidelity. Here we are in the realm of pathology, of psychosis. Suspicion is at once sublimed into a certainty that shakes not only the sufferer and his victims but the language itself. It is the more extraordinary that for so long critics could speak of these final plays as the work of a man who had triumphed over many difficulties and was now gentle and contented. One instance of tortured language must serve: Leontes is with his son Mamillius, brooding on his wife's supposed adultery with his friend Polixenes, King of Bohemia:

> There have been
> (Or I am much deceiv'd) cuckolds ere now,
> And many a man there is (even at this present,
> Now, while I speak this) holds his wife by th' arm,
> That little thinks she has been sluic'd in's absence,
> And his pond fish'd by his next neighbour – by
> Sir Smile, his neighbour. Nay, there's comfort in't,
> Whiles other men have gates, and those gates open'd,
> As mine, against their will. Should all despair
> That have revolted wives, the tenth of mankind
> Would hang themselves. Physic for't there's none;
> It is a bawdy planet, that will strike
> Where 'tis predominant; and 'tis powerful – think it –
> From east, west, north and south. Be it concluded,
> No barricado for a belly. Know't,
> It will let in and out the enemy
> With bag and baggage. Many thousands on's
> Have the disease, and feel't not.
>
> (I.ii.190–207)

This rant, steeped in sexual disgust, continues almost to the point in the plot where – after the trial, the death of the son (the little boy who has stood bewildered through the outburst just quoted), and the report of Hermione's death – Leontes finally accepts the truth of the oracle affirming her innocence. By that time the daughter she bore has been cast away on the 'coast of

Bohemia' and found by shepherds. Now sixteen years pass, and there follows the long pastoral act; the child, Perdita, now grown up, is a shepherdess loved by Florizel, the son of Polixenes.

It may seem superfluous to praise Shakespeare on his skill and intelligence, but in this part of the play, in such contrast with the pathological rage of the opening acts, everything except the attitude of Polixenes to the union of Perdita and Florizel is calm and lively: the exquisite conversation of the lovers; the vital difference of opinion between Perdita and Polixenes on art and nature, the central topic of the play; the comic dialogue of the shepherds; and the antics of the rural con man Autolycus.

The great moment is the statue scene at the end: 'O royal piece, / There's magic in thy majesty', says Leontes (V.iii.38–9), while Perdita stands 'like stone' (V.iii.42) beside her mother, now no longer stone. What could be more admirable than the words of Leontes when he sees the stone statue come to life: 'What fine chisel / Could ever yet cut breath?' (78–9)? One could say of this scene what Leontes says of the statue: 'If this be magic, let it be an art / Lawful as eating' (110–11). The statue becomes a queen, made not by art but by the hand of 'great creating nature' (IV.iv.88). Based on Greene's unremarkable tale, the play is itself a triumph of art. Those who find signs of relaxation or resignation in the poet of this period are missing the abundant evidence of his great energy. Perhaps they also forget that Shakespeare was about forty-six when he wrote it – hardly an age, even in the seventeenth century, for retreat to sheltered accommodation.

The last of the plays attributable wholly or mainly to Shakespeare is *The Tempest*. Of all his works this was the most obviously influenced by the prospect of performance at the Blackfriars, and by the courtly entertainments in which the company was from time to time involved. This is not to say it was not performed at the Globe, but it is well adapted to performance in locations with more resources for the staging of spectacle. We know it was played at court, probably in the Banqueting House in Whitehall in 1611 and later during the celebrations of the betrothal of James's daughter Elizabeth to the Elector Palatine in 1612. The Stuart court is famous for its masques, but although it is usual to refer to the entertainment offered by Prospero in IV.i as a masque it is really only a pseudo-masque, for the true masque must end with dancing in which both masquers and audience participate, and it commonly contained an elaborate allegorical message as well as a fulsome tribute to the royal person presiding. The Banqueting House, later rebuilt by Inigo Jones, may still be seen in Whitehall, with its vast allegorical ceiling paintings by Rubens; it has the additional interest that Charles I emerged from it onto the scaffold where he was beheaded in 1649. The masque as a form of drama was almost indissolubly associated with the absolutist aspirations of the Stuarts, so there was a certain rather appalling propriety in his enemies' choice of this site. By 1649 the theatres had been closed (by opponents of Charles) for a good many years; but the passion for spectacle and drama, present throughout the narrative of the early English theatre, had not died, only moved outside; 'scaffold' was a word for a playing-place as well as for the ritual of public execution, and Marvell was right to describe Charles, on this occasion, as 'the royal actor'.

Once again it is necessary to remind oneself that *The Tempest*, though a romance, ending in betrothal and the partial reconciliation of old enemies, is far from being a gentle play. Much of the language is rough late Shakespeare, with minimal pauses at the ends of lines, and metaphors which flash by like meteors:

> Thy false uncle…
> Being once perfected how to grant suits,
> How to deny them, who t'advance, and who
> To trash for overtopping, new created
> The creatures that were mine, I say, or chang'd 'em,
> Or else new-form'd 'em; having both the key
> Of officer and office, set all hearts i' th' state
> To what tune pleas'd his ear, that now he was
> The ivy which had hid my princely trunk,
> And suck'd my verdure out on't.
>
> (I.ii.77–87)

This is Prospero explaining to Miranda, with mixed metaphors that indicate his perturbation at the memory, the usurpation of his dukedom by his brother Antonio. Prospero has to recount at length to his daughter, who is said to have known nothing of them, the circumstances of his and her exile, and his excited way of doing so is a way of enlivening an old-fashioned bit of exposition. It is placed where it is, at the moment when at last Prospero has his enemies at his mercy, as a more conventionally dramatic solution to the problem solved in *The Winter's Tale* by having a gap between the events that caused the trouble and the solution of them a generation later. As an exposition it is a bit awkward, since there is so little for Miranda to say except to reassure her irritable father that she is indeed listening carefully to him. However, by the end of the scene we have been well informed, not only about the treachery of

Antonio and the goodness of Gonzalo, but about the characters of Ariel, Caliban, and Ferdinand, who, despite his apparently hopeless plight, has already 'chang'd eyes' with Miranda (I.ii.442).

The romance plot is no longer random, for it is subject to the will and direction of Prospero, who stages the whole thing from the storm on and is about to perform his final tricks. He will retire from being a mage, returning from a solitary life of scholarship to the active sphere of government from which his brother's treachery, compounded by his own neglect, had expelled him.

The play is one of the shortest in the canon, with much of Act IV devoted to the masque, which has no narrative value; but a good deal happens within its compass. Once again, the audience will have been aware of watching an old romance given very unusual, modern treatment. The most pleasing verse is given to the non-human characters Caliban and Ariel, though Ferdinand's speech 'This music crept by me upon the waters' (I.ii.392) and Alonso's outburst of grief at the supposed death of his son (III.iii.95–102) are fine. The most intensely written scene describes the conspiracy between Antonio and Sebastian to kill Alonso; it almost brings back the mood of *Macbeth*: 'My strong imagination sees a crown / Dropping upon thy head' (II.i.208–9). The final reconciliations, said to be the work of Providence, allow certain notes that roughen the harmony. Prospero himself is distinctly ungentle, calling Antonio 'most wicked sir, whom to call brother / Would even infect my mouth' (V.i.130–1). Antonio remains silent, as if indifferent to this harsh act of forgiveness. Caliban, an updated version of the medieval Wild Man, now associated with the natives of the New World – a victim of a mistaken educational policy – ends the play a tamed revolutionary who will in future know not to tangle with his colonial masters.

There is no doubt that Shakespeare would be well aware of the doings of the Virginia Company, an important contemporary commercial venture; and he appears to have seen William Strachey's report of the wreck of one of the Company's ships in 1610, not published until later. But the 'colonialist' programme of *The Tempest* has been too much exploited. The allusion to 'the still-vex'd Bermoothes' (I.ii.229) has made people forget that Alonso's ship is wrecked on a Mediterranean island and Ariel, in mentioning the Bermudas, is merely trying to emphasize how far away they were. No doubt Caliban mixes some traditional European characteristics (the Wild Man or Wodwose) with features of the New World 'Indian' as reported by Montaigne and others, but the play is set in the Old World. Attempts to relate its action to high European politics also lack foundation; much has been made of its performance during the betrothal celebrations of the Princess, but it was one among many in a list that included *Othello*.

Indeed, this play has been the subject of much vain speculation. It has been claimed for Masonry, held to enact Greek initiation ceremonies. It has been compared (more understandably) with Mozart's *Magic Flute*. The Epilogue has won the most fanciful treatment, for it is thought to relate to the playwright's imminent retirement from the theatre. There is admittedly quite a good fit between the resignations of a magician and a dramatist, but Epilogues were not used in this way. Not many have survived, but in those that do, it is usual for the speaker to allude as wittily as possible to the play and to his or her part in it (compare Rosalind in *As You Like It* and the Chorus in *Henry V*). The epilogue has always been a request for applause, and that is what we have at the end of *The Tempest:* 'release me from my bands / With the help of your good hands' (9–10), with some apt references to seafaring and magic mixed in.

In any case Shakespeare did not give up work. He collaborated with Fletcher on the lost play *Cardenio,* on *The Two Noble Kinsmen,* and on *Henry VIII.* The latter represented an ambitious return to the English history that had occupied him for so long in the past, and to the still immediately important subject of Elizabeth's father (and King James's kinsman), whose many marriages offered no long-term solution to problems of succession; these were solved only, if indeed they truly were, at the Queen's death in 1603.

Shakespeare was not yet fifty – he had lived half a century in times of great change and some danger; he had had very considerable commercial success, and may well have intended to go on enjoying it. In 1608 he had pledged himself to pay his share of the Blackfriars rent for twenty-one years, and in 1613 he bought a London house, the gatehouse of the former Blackfriars monastery. Perhaps this was an investment, but men about to retire rarely buy property next door to their place of work, and the purchase more probably signified an intention to stay active in the adjoining theatre. He did spend more time in Stratford, perhaps for family reasons, perhaps to attend to his many business interests there. Possibly at some point he found a tenant for the Blackfriars gatehouse. It is sometimes suggested that he went home because he was old and/or ill; but he was not old, and we know nothing whatever to suggest that he was ill.

Shakespeare was evidently a man who looked after his money, and his share in theatre profits, together with income from property in Warwickshire, left him and his heirs wealthy. He was also somewhat litigious, as some rich men are. His colleagues, co-lessors of the Blackfriars, and sharers in the Globe (which was rebuilt after the fire of 1613), were also well off. The theatrical profession, which barely existed when Shakespeare was born, could now make men rich.

The theatres continued to flourish, with powerful new playwrights – Fletcher, Webster, Massinger, Ford and Middleton all worked for the King's Men – while the political atmosphere darkened. Margot Heinemann notes that 'A new form of history play, prudently set in Italy, France, or Spain, dealt with spies and informers, driven by poverty and lack of political preferment ... rulers [were] shown as corrupt or even mad, aided by unscrupulous churchmen,' as in Webster's *Duchess of Malfi*.

The financial difficulties of the King worsened; his parliaments were hostile, their dislike of him exacerbated by his absolutist pretensions, his passion for favourites, his importation of many Scotsmen, and his selling of titles, including that of baronet, an obsolete rank he reinvented for the purpose. Fear of Catholic subversion, which haunted English history for centuries, grew more active after the Gunpowder Plot. James, who was the son of a notoriously Catholic mother and the husband of a Catholic princess, tried to arrange a marriage between his heir, Charles, and a Spanish princess, who was of course Catholic. On the other religious wing, the Puritan clergy were permanently disaffected. Now and again the theatre took a more direct interest in these political issues. Middleton's play *A Game at Chess* (1624), a political allegory concerning the proposed Spanish marriage, enjoyed great success on stage and in print. It ran for nine consecutive days at the Globe and drew great crowds before it was suppressed. Hunter wonders why it was licensed in the first place, why it ran so long before action was taken, and why it was printed without interference; the suspicion is that 'some powerful faction at court' protected it or perhaps even set it up. Certainly it has a more direct bearing on contemporary politics – the relations with Spain and the papacy, and more generally between Protestantism and Catholicism – than any of Shakespeare's plays. Hunter may be right in scenting a 'change in cultural sensibility'. Charles I eventually married a Catholic princess, and later his nephew, the Catholic James II, would reap the whirlwind sown by the Stuart interest in the old faith.

Meanwhile, as usual, the distribution of wealth ensured that the poor got poorer, and society became more divided and more violent. As the population expanded so did the numbers of unemployed, while in the City, fortunes were made by men such as the extortioner and monopolist Giles Mompesson, portrayed in Massinger's play *A New Way to Pay Old Debts* (1621) as Sir Giles Overreach. London now being a very large financial centre, criminal greed was only to be expected; however, Mompesson was publicly disgraced.

Such were some of the problems, ecclesiastical, economic and social, that reached their climax in 1642, the year in which Charles Stuart began his progress to the block and England prepared itself for an experiment in republicanism. It was also in 1642 that Parliament closed the theatres, and they stayed closed until the Restoration, when they returned in very altered form. The history of Shakespeare and his company, indeed the great age of English drama, ends there.

Notes

References to passages from Shakespeare quoted in the text are to the Riverside edition, ed. Gwynne Blakemore Evans (2nd ed., 1997). Square brackets in the text, indicating deviations from the copy text, are here omitted.

P. 2, L. 1. *How many plays were written... have survived:* G. K. Hunter, *English Drama 1586–1942* (1997), p. 2.

P. 3, L. 26. *'rogues, vagabonds... baron of this realm':* A. Gurr, *The Shakespearean Stage* (1992), p. 27.

P. 12, L. 16. *'The rhythms of the liturgy... of life itself':* Duffy, *The Stripping of the Altars* (1992), p. 52.

P. 17, L. 13. *'the largest confiscation... since the Norman Conquest':* John Guy, *Tudor England* (1988), p. 149.

P. 24, L. 20. *'the strangest variety... solitary and unmarried':* Francis Bacon, *Advancement of Learning*, Book 2 (1605). Bacon returned to this idea several times.

P. 27, L. 20. *'And for the vanities... after their death were opened':* extracted in J. Dover Wilson, ed., *Life in Shakespeare's England* (1944), p. 148.

P. 28, L. 10. *'For a man... by profession':* T.G., *The Rich Cabinet* (1616), in Wilson, *Life in Shakespeare's England*, p. 224.

P. 33, L. 1. *'Surely... his daughter Elizabeth':* Peter Milward, 'Religion in Arden', *Shakespeare Survey* 54 (2001), p. 121.

P. 33, L. 17. *the case for Shakespeare as a Protestant... religious adherence:* David Daniell, 'Shakespeare and the Protestant Mind', *Shakespeare Survey* 54 (2001), pp. 1–12.

P. 38, L. 19. *it is known... 'a generation and a half':* John Guy, *Tudor England*, p. 416.

P. 41, L. 7. *A foreign visitor…by the Thames:* Paul Hentzner, *A Journey into England…in 1598,* quoted by T. F. Reddaway in 'London and the Court', *Shakespeare Survey* 17 (1964), p. 3.

P. 42, L. 15. *One should add…bad characters:* Guy, *Tudor England,* p. 326.

P. 44, L. 3. *special performance:* It has recently been argued that the play put on by Shakespeare's company was not Shakespeare's but a dramatized version of Hayward's book. This seems to me very unlikely. The case is too complex to argue here, but as the new theory would affect the argument if it were true, I mention it here (Blair Worden, 'Which play was performed at the Globe Theatre on 7 February 1601', *London Review of Books,* July 10, 2003).

P. 49, L. 4. *'the court was…tells its own story':* Dominic Baker-Smith, 'Shakespeare and the Court', in *The Court Historian* 6 (2001), p. 94.

P. 51, L. 11. *'to warn…mean to set forth':* quoted in Gurr, *The Shakespearean Stage, 1574–1642,* 3rd ed. (1993), p. 73.

P. 53, L. 14. *'tonal variety':* Peter Thomson, *Shakespeare's Professional Career* (1992), p. 108.

P. 54, L. 15. *the good actor should… 'the person personated':* Gurr, p. 99.

P. 61, L. 16. *'Sour wit…traits of the revenger':* John Kerrigan, *Revenge Tragedy* (1996), pp. 196ff.

P. 62, L. 17. *The scholars of the Inn…dramatic structure:* For the classical sources see Geoffrey Bullough, *Narrative and Dramatic Sources of Shakespeare,* 8 vols (1957–75), vol. 1, pp. 7–9.

P. 63, L. 9. *'measures the whole story…individual experience':* G. K. Hunter, *English Drama 1586–1642: The Age of Shakespeare* (1997), pp. 118–19.

P. 69, L. 9. *'cultured, if playful…amorous intrigues':* Anthony Holden, *William Shakespeare* (1999), p. 122.

P. 82, L. 18. *'The Merry Wives…let's hear Verdi':* W. H. Auden, *Lectures on Shakespeare,* ed. Arthur Kirsch (2000), p. 124.

P. 83, L. 12. *'ideas about the Jews…national difference':* James Shapiro, *Shakespeare and the Jews* (1996), p. 2.

P. 89, L. 23. *puts it mildly... debatable:* Gurr, pp. 132–36.

P. 91, L. 8. *'more than a third... a house in Stratford':* Gurr, p. 194.

P. 95, L. 3. *'a house... Shakespeare and others':* Park Honan, *Shakespeare: A Life* (1998), p. 268.

P. 98, L. 17. *'Daily at two... refreshment':* Gurr, p. 214.

P. 101, L. 2. *'what remains obscure... something of value':* C. S. Lewis, *English Literature of the Sixteenth Century, Excluding Drama* (1954), p. 511.

P. 104, L. 5. *'bizarre... comic toadies':* Hunter, p. 308.

P. 108, L. 10. *'That the academic term... to describe it':* Gurr, p. 99.

P. 112, L. 11. *'riddled with... its new theatre':* Holden, pp. 171, 176.

P. 116, L. 17. *every Elizabethan schoolboy...* Gallic Wars: T.J.B. Spencer, 'Shakespeare: The Roman Plays', in B. Dobrée, ed., *Shakespeare: The Writer and His Work* (1964), p. 304.

L. 20. *Ben Jonson... eliminate the mistake:* See Ian Donaldson, ed., *Ben Jonson* (The Oxford Authors, 1985), p. 540.

P. 124, L. 11. *'the first... in some things':* Donaldson, p. 397.

P. 133, L. 26. *'loosely to... many Europeans':* Honigmann, ed., *Othello* (Arden edn., 1997), p. 15.

P. 137, L. 16. *'it also shows... active evil':* Hunter, p. 494.

P. 177, L. 10. *'A new form... unscrupulous churchmen':* Margot Heinemann, 'Political Drama', in A. R. Braunmuller and Michael Hattaway, *The Cambridge Companion to Renaissance Drama* (1990), pp. 161–206, p. 190.

P. 178, L. 4. *'some powerful faction at court':* Hunter, pp. 491–2.
L. 9. *'change in cultural sensibility':* Hunter, *ibid.*

Bibliographical Note

This list is inevitably selective. It includes some works because they are regarded as standard, and others because they seem to me particularly instructive.

For the dramatic aspects of late-medieval religion and culture see Eamon Duffy, *The Stripping of the Altars* (1992). The 'theatre of state power', and the continuation in the subsequent period of the practice of dramatizing such events as executions, is treated at length in Peter Lake, *The Antichrist's Lewd Hat* (2002). The bibliographies provided in these books give access to quantities of information.

For the Corpus Christi or mystery cycles of plays see Richard Beadle, *The Cambridge Companion to Medieval English Theatre* (1994) and Marianne C. Briscoe and John C. Coldewey, eds, *Contexts for Early English Drama* (1989).

For the general history of the Tudor period, and more particularly of the reign of Elizabeth I, see John Guy, *Tudor England* (1988), John Guy, ed., *The Tudor Monarchy* (1997), Christopher Haigh, *Elizabeth I* (1988), and Colin Burrow, 'The Sixteenth Century', in Arthur F. Kinney, ed., *The Cambridge Companion to English Literature, 1500–1600* (2000), pp. 11–28. For Elizabeth's own writings, or some of them, see Leah S. Marcus, Janet Mueller, and Mary Beth Rose, *Elizabeth I: Collected Works* (2000).

The vagaries of patronage are illuminated by Phoebe Sheavyn's *The Literary Profession in the Elizabethan Age* (2nd edn., revised by J. W. Saunders, 1967). An excellent short account is given by Catherine Bates in 'Poetry, Patronage and the Court', including an up-to-date bibliography, in Kinney, *Cambridge Companion*, pp. 90–103. An early standard work on the more popular kinds of writing is Louis B. Wright, *Middle-Class Culture in Elizabethan England* (1935); see also A. V. Judge, ed., *The Elizabethan Underworld* (1930) and Arthur F. Kinney, *Rogues, Vagabonds and Sturdy Beggars* (1972).

The influence of printing on the intellectual life of the time, theological, literary and scientific, is the subject of Elizabeth L. Eisenstein's now classic *The Printing Revolution in Early Modern Europe* (1983). The rise of conspicuous consumption during the Renaissance is the subject of Lisa Jardine's *Worldly Goods* (1996).

On the culture and conditions of life in Shakespeare's time, the two-volume tercentenary *Shakespeare's England* (1916), subtitled 'An Account of the Life and Manners of His Age', is still a most valuable source. It has chapters by the leading scholars of the time on religion, the court, the army, the navy, exploration, travel, scholarship, commerce and coinage, agriculture, law, medicine, the sciences, the arts, heraldry, costume, bookselling, actors and acting, playhouses, sport (hunting, falconry, coursing), archery, horse-manship, bear-baiting, dancing, and rogues and vagabonds. In detail some of the material may have been superseded, but no one book has so much relevant information on the age. A small but valuable supplement to it is John Dover Wilson's anthology *Life in Shakespeare's England* (1911, reprinted as a Penguin book in 1944 and subsequently). Over the years the annual *Shakespeare Survey* has augmented the information and discussions of *Shakespeare's England*; see especially volume 17 of 1964. Another useful book is Alan and Veronica Palmer's *Who's Who in Shakespeare's England* (2000), which includes short biographies of officers of state as well as of writers and dramatists and has a useful glossary explaining such terms as 'recusant'.

The work of E. K. Chambers is often the foundation of later work on Shakespeare, and his *William Shakespeare: A Study of Facts and Problems* (1930) is still necessary. More modern biographies include Samuel Schoenbaum's excellent *William Shakespeare: A Documentary Life* (1975), Park Honan's *Shakespeare: A Life* (1998), Katherine Duncan-Jones's *Ungentle Shakespeare* (2001), and, in a more popular tone, Anthony Holden's *William Shakespeare* (1999). These books incorporate the biographical discoveries of many determined scholars too numerous to be mentioned here, but an exception should be made for Ernest A. Honigmann, a bold and original researcher who was largely responsible for, among other things, the idea at present enjoying a vogue that Shakespeare, as a young man, served in a Catholic household in Lancashire before turning up in London in 1592. Honigmann's relevant books are

Shakespeare: The 'Lost Years' (1985, rev. 1998), and *Shakespeare's Impact on His Contemporaries* (1982).

A magisterial overview of the drama of the entire period is G. K. Hunter's *English Drama 1586–1642: The Age of Shakespeare* (1997). (In an earlier volume of the *Oxford History of English Literature*, published in 1969, Hunter had completed F. P. Wilson's study of the drama from 1485 to 1585.)

There is an actively growing literature on the playhouses of the period, and E. K. Chambers, *The Elizabethan Stage* (4 vols, 1923), though an important foundation, is now in some respects out of date. See Glynne Wickham, *Early English Stages*, vol. 2, parts 1 and 2 (1963, 1972). Philip Henslowe's *Diary* is edited by R. A. Foakes and R. T. Rickert (1961). Numerous studies are devoted to particular playhouses, and the Globe has naturally had more attention than the others. Andrew Gurr's *The Shakespearean Stage, 1574–1632* (3rd ed., 1992) is virtually indispensable; see also his *Playgoing in Shakespeare's London* (1987). Peter Thomson, *Shakespeare's Professional Career* (1992) is lively and instructive. R. A. Foakes provides a useful short account of the playhouses in 'Playhouses and Players', included in A. R. Braunmuller and Michael Hattaway, *The Cambridge Companion to English Renaissance Drama* (1990). The Blackfriars theatre (often called 'the second Blackfriars' when the topic is the tenancy of Shakespeare's company) is studied in Herbert Berry, *Shakespeare's Playhouses* (1987) and Irwin Smith, *Shakespeare's Blackfriars Playhouse* (1964); see also Gurr, above.

Other books about the theatres and their companies are Bernard Beckerman's *Shakespeare at the Globe, 1599–1609* (1962), among other virtues good on acting, a topic formerly disputed between B. L. Joseph, *Elizabethan Acting* (1951) and Marvin Rosenberg, 'Elizabethan Actors: Men or Marionettes?' in *PMLA* (1954). Among several pioneering books by Muriel C. Bradbrook are *Elizabethan Stage Conditions* (1932) and *The Rise of the Common Player* (1962). T. W. Baldwin's *The Organization and Personnel of the Shakespearean Company* (1927) is another important pioneer. The boys' companies have attracted special studies: Reavley Gair, *The Children of St Paul's* (1982) is very useful.

Several studies are dedicated to the role of the Fool; they originate with Enid Welsford's study of that title (1935), complemented by R. H. Goldsmith, *Wise Fools in Shakespeare*

(1935). The theme is developed with allusion to particular performers by David Wiles, *Shakespeare's Clown* (1987). The jig at the end of the show is the subject of C. R. Baskerville's monograph *The Elizabethan Jig* (1929). Music, which was always needed but grew more subtle and important at the Blackfriars, is the subject of F. W. Sternfeld, *Music in Shakespearean Tragedy* (1963). See also Steven Mullaney, *The Place of the Stage* (1988).

Many studies exist of the political implications of the drama – to name a few, Margot Heinemann's *Puritanism and Theatre* (1980), Jonathan Dollimore and Alan Sinfield's *Political Shakespeare* (1985), David Norbrook's *Poetry and Politics in the English Renaissance* (1984), and Stephen Orgel's *The Illusion of Power* (1975).

Studies of the character of the Elizabethan audience include Alfred Harbage, *Shakespeare's Audience* (1941) and *Shakespeare and the Rival Traditions* (1952). Harbage maintained that Shakespeare's audience consisted largely of the artisan class; for a view of the audience as made up of more privileged people see Ann Jennalie Cook, *The Privileged Playgoers of Shakespeare's London* (1981). Both views are assessed by Gurr in his *Playgoing in Shakespeare's London* (1987).

Index